MUNITORUM FIELD MANUAL

POINTS VALUES FOR WARHAMMER 40,000

D0662612

CONTENTS

Introduction 3

Adeptus Astartes 4
Space Marines 4
Black Templars 6
Ultramarines 6
White Scars 6
Iron Hands 6
Imperial Fists 6
Salamanders 6
Raven Guard 6
Blood Angels 7
Dark Angels 9
Space Wolves 11
Deathwatch 14
Grey Knights 15

Forces of the Imperium 16
Adepta Sororitas 16
Adeptus Custodes 17
Sisters of Silence 18
Officio Assassinorum 18
Astra Militarum 18
Adeptus Mechanicus 20
Imperial Knights 21
Inquisition 22

Forces of Chaos.................................... 22
Chaos Space Marines 22
Death Guard 24
Thousand Sons 25
Chaos Daemons 28
Chaos Knights 29

Forces of the Xenos................................. 29
Craftworlds..29
Drukhari 30
Harlequins 32
Ynnari..32

Necrons 32
Orks..33
T'au Empire 36
Tyranids 38
Genestealer Cults 39

Unaligned Fortifications 40

Forge World Points Values 42
Adeptus Astartes...42
Grey Knights 43
Inquisition 43
Adeptus Custodes 44
Adeptus Mechanicus 44
Astra Militarum 46
Death Korps of Krieg 47
Questor Imperialis 48
Titan Legions 48
Daemon Bound 49
Hellforged 49
Lords of Ruin 50
Heretic Titan Legions..50
Eyrine Cults 50
Children of the Warp 50
Questor Traitoris 51
Asuryani 51
Drukhari 52
Necrons 52
Orks..54
T'au Empire 54
Tyranids 55

Miscellaneous Points Values 56
Gellerpox Infected 56
Elucidian Starstriders..56
Imperium...56
Blackstone Fortress..56
Indomitus Set 56

PRODUCED BY THE WARHAMMER STUDIO

With thanks to the Mournival for their additional playtesting services

Munitorum Field Manual © Copyright Games Workshop Limited 2020. Munitorum Field Manual, GW, Games Workshop, Space Marine, 40K, Warhammer, Warhammer 40,000, the 'Aquila' Double-headed Eagle logo, and all associated logos, illustrations, images, names, creatures, races, vehicles, locations, weapons, characters, and the distinctive likenesses thereof, are either ® or TM, and/or © Games Workshop Limited, variably registered around the world. All Rights Reserved.

Games Workshop Ltd, Willow Rd, Lenton, Nottingham, NG7 2WS
games-workshop.com

INTRODUCTION

Welcome to the 2020 edition of the Munitorum Field Manual. This book contains the most up-to-date points values that should be used in your matched play games, covering all the factions in Warhammer 40,000.

Since we have written the latest edition of Warhammer 40,000 we have been working tirelessly to review and update the points values for every single, model, weapon and item of wargear in the 41st Millennium.

Whilst it has not been a year since we last did a points review, we felt it vital to do so now to take account of all the changes introduced with the latest edition of Warhammer 40,000. For example, we have introduced dedicated matched play mission packs, created Blast weapons, overhauled how battlefields and terrain function, and let's not forget that vehicles and monsters have become substantially better – being able to move and fire heavy weapons at full effect, and even shoot while enemy models are within Engagement Range of them! I'm sure you can see that together, these changes affect the relative efficacy of certain models and weapons, hence the need for a review.

Before I go further, I should mention that this monolithic task would have been impossible without the dedication and stalwart advice of our playtesting teams, in particular the adepts of the Mournival across the world, who have our eternal thanks.

The points values listed in this book replace any published previously, and should be used in your matched play games (or any of your games that are using points values). As with the previous edition of the Munitorum Field Manual, this book contains the points values for every single model and item of wargear that, at the time of printing, are supported for matched play games, eliminating the need to flip back and forth between two or more books.

I hope that you are enjoying the latest edition of Warhammer 40,000, and we wish you luck on the battlefield.

- Robin Cruddace and the
Warhammer 40,000 Rules Team

Note that a weapon can appear in several different lists, each with a different points cost (for example, meltaguns appear in both the Space Marines and Astra Militarum lists). If such an item of wargear appears in one of the tables in this book, that points value only applies to the appropriate faction.

Also note that your army cannot include the same named character more than once.

ADEPTUS ASTARTES

SPACE MARINES

HQ	MODELS/UNIT	POINTS/MODEL*
Captain	1	80
Captain with Jump Pack	1	105
Captain in Cataphractii Armour	1	95
Captain in Gravis Armour	1	105
Captain in Phobos Armour	1	93
Captain in Terminator Armour	1	95
Captain on Bike	1	100
Chaplain	1	80
Chaplain with Jump Pack	1	105
Chaplain in Terminator Armour	1	95
Librarian	1	90
Librarian with Jump Pack	1	115
Librarian in Phobos Armour	1	98
Librarian in Terminator Armour	1	105
Lieutenants	1-2	65
- with Jump Packs		90
Lieutenants in Phobos Armour	1-2	78
Primaris Captain	1	85
Primaris Chaplain	1	85
Primaris Librarian	1	95
Primaris Lieutenants	1-2	70
Techmarine	1	40

TROOPS	MODELS/UNIT	POINTS/MODEL*
Incursor Squad	5-10	21
Infiltrator Squad	5-10	24 (Infiltrator Helix Adept is 34)
Intercessor Squad	5-10	20
Scout Squad	5-10	14
Tactical Squad	5-10	15

ELITES	MODELS/UNIT	POINTS/MODEL*
Aggressor Squad	3-6	40
Ancient in Terminator Armour	1	90
Apothecary	1	55
Cataphractii Terminator Squad	5-10	26
Centurion Assault Squad	3-6	45
Company Ancient	1	75
Company Champion	1	40
Company Veterans	2-5	17
Contemptor Dreadnought	1	105
Dreadnought	1	70
Invictor Tactical Warsuit	1	135
Ironclad Dreadnought	1	70
Primaris Ancient	1	80
Primaris Apothecary	1	60
Redemptor Dreadnought	1	125
Reiver Squad	5-10	18
Servitors	4	7
Sternguard Veteran Squad	5-10	17
Tartaros Terminator Squad	5-10	23
Terminator Assault Squad	5-10	23
Terminator Squad	5-10	23

ELITES	MODELS/UNIT	POINTS/MODEL*
Vanguard Veteran Squad	5-10	17
Vanguard Veteran Squad with Jump Packs	5-10	19
Venerable Dreadnought	1	85

FAST ATTACK	MODELS/UNIT	POINTS/MODEL*
Assault Squad	5-10	15
Assault Squad with Jump Packs	5-10	17
Attack Bike Squad	1-3	30
Bike Squad	3-8	25
- Attack Bike	0-1	30
Inceptor Squad	3-6	40
Land Speeders	1-3	45
Scout Bike Squad	3-9	25
Suppressor Squad	3	33

HEAVY SUPPORT	MODELS/UNIT	POINTS/MODEL*
Centurion Devastator Squad	3-6	60
Devastator Squad	5-10	15
Eliminator Squad	3	28
Hellblaster Squad	5-10	33
Hunter	1	95
Land Raider	1	175
Land Raider Crusader	1	215
Land Raider Redeemer	1	240
Predator	1	90
Repulsor Executioner	1	250
Stalker	1	95
Thunderfire Cannon	1	85
- Techmarine Gunner	1	45
Vindicator	1	130
Whirlwind	1	125

DEDICATED TRANSPORTS	MODELS/UNIT	POINTS/MODEL*
Drop Pod	1	65
Impulsor	1	100
Land Speeder Storm	1	40
Razorback	1	80
Repulsor	1	230
Rhino	1	75

FLYERS	MODELS/UNIT	POINTS/MODEL*
Stormhawk Interceptor	1	115
Stormraven Gunship	1	240
Stormtalon Gunship	1	105

* Excluding wargear
** Including wargear

RANGED WEAPONS	POINTS/WEAPON	RANGED WEAPONS	POINTS/WEAPON
Absolvor bolt pistol	0	Master-crafted stalker bolt rifle	5
Accelerator autocannon	0	Melta bombs	5
Assault bolter	0	Meltagun	10
Assault cannon (INFANTRY/other model)	15/20	Missile launcher (INFANTRY/other model)	15/20
Assault plasma incinerator	0	Multi-melta (INFANTRY/other model)	20/25
Astartes grenade launcher	0	Occulus bolt carbine	0
Astartes shotgun	0	Onslaught gatling cannon	20
Auto bolt rifle	0	Plasma blaster	10
Auto boltstorm gauntlets	0	Plasma cannon	15
Bellicatus missile array	20	Plasma cutter	5
Bolt carbine	0	Plasma exterminator	5
Bolt pistol	0	Plasma gun	10
Bolt rifle	0	Plasma incinerator	0
Bolt sniper rifle	0	Plasma pistol	5
Boltgun	0	Predator autocannon	40
Boltstorm gauntlet	0	Reaper autocannon	10
Centurion missile launcher	15	Reductor pistol	0
Cerberus launcher	0	Shock grenades	0
Combi-bolter	3	Skyhammer missile launcher	20
Combi-flamer	10	Skyspear missile launcher	0
Combi-grav	10	Sniper rifle	2
Combi-melta	10	Special issue boltgun	0
Combi-plasma	10	Stalker bolt rifle	0
Cyclone missile launcher	25	Storm bolter	3
Deathwind launcher	5	Stormstrike missile launcher	0
Demolisher cannon	0	Thunderfire cannon	0
Flamer	5	Twin assault cannon	40
Flamestorm cannon	0	Twin boltgun	0
Flamestorm gauntlets	0	Twin heavy bolter	30
Frag grenades	0	Twin heavy plasma cannon	40
Fragstorm grenade launcher	5	Twin Icarus ironhail heavy stubber	0
Grav-cannon and grav-amp (INFANTRY/other model)	10/15	Twin ironhail autocannon	0
Grav-gun	10	Twin lascannon	40
Grav-pistol	5	Twin multi-melta	50
Grenade harness	5	Typhoon missile launcher	40
Hand flamer	5	Volkite charger	5
Heavy bolt pistol	0	Whirlwind castellan launcher	0
Heavy bolter (INFANTRY/other model)	10/15	Whirlwind vengeance launcher	10
Heavy flamer (INFANTRY/other model)	10/15	Wrist-mounted grenade launcher	0
Heavy laser destroyer	40		
Heavy onslaught gatling cannon	30		
Heavy plasma cannon	20		
Heavy plasma incinerator	0		
Hunter-killer missile	5		
Hurricane bolter	15		
Icarus ironhail heavy stubber	5		
Icarus rocket pod	5		
Icarus stormcannon	10		
Incendium cannon	0		
Instigator bolt carbine	0		
Ironhail heavy stubber	5		
Ironhail skytalon array	5		
Kheres-pattern assault cannon	25		
Krak grenades	0		
Krakstorm grenade launcher	5		
Las fusil	10		
Las-talon	35		
Lascannon (INFANTRY/other model)	15/20		
Macro plasma incinerator	30		
Marksman bolt carbine	0		
Master-crafted auto bolt rifle	5		
Master-crafted boltgun	5		
Master-crafted instigator bolt carbine	5		
Master-crafted occulus bolt carbine	0		

OTHER WARGEAR	POINTS/ITEM
Armorium Cherub	5
Auto launchers	0
Auxiliary grenade launcher	2
Camo cloak	2
Centurion assault launchers	0
Combat shield	3
Grapnel launcher	2
Grav-chute	2
Haywire mine	10
Infiltrator comms array	5
Ironclad assault launchers	5
Shield dome	25
Smoke grenades	0
Orbital comms array	20
Storm shield (CHARACTER/other model)	10/4
Teleport homer	5

MELEE WEAPONS	POINTS/WEAPON
Chainfist	10
Chainsword	0
Combat knife	0
Crozius arcanum	0
Dreadnought chainfist	30
Dreadnought combat weapon	20
Invictor fist	0
Eviscerator	10
Force axe	0
Force stave	0
Force sword	0
Lightning claws (single/pair)	5/10
Master-crafted power sword	10
Paired combat blades	0
Power axe	5
Power fist	10
Power maul	5
Power sword	5
Redemptor fist	0
Relic blade	10
Seismic hammer	30
Servo-arm	0
Siege drills	0
Thunder hammer (CHARACTER/other model)	40/15

BLACK TEMPLARS

NAMED CHARACTERS	MODELS/UNIT	POINTS/MODEL**
High Marshal Helbrecht	1	155
The Emperor's Champion	1	80
Chaplain Grimaldus	1	95

TROOPS	MODELS/UNIT	POINTS/MODEL*
Crusader Squad	5-20	15 (Neophyte is 14)

ELITES	MODELS/UNIT	POINTS/MODEL*
Cenobyte Servitors	3	6

ULTRAMARINES

NAMED CHARACTERS	MODELS/UNIT	POINTS/MODEL**
Captain Sicarius	1	115
Chaplain Cassius	1	95
Chief Librarian Tigurius	1	135
Marneus Calgar	1	210
Roboute Guilliman	1	380
Sergeant Chronus	1	35
Sergeant Telion	1	70

ELITES	MODELS/UNIT	POINTS/MODEL**
Chapter Ancient	1	100
Chapter Champion	1	75
Honour Guard	2	25
Tyrannic War Veterans	4-10	17
Victrix Honour Guard	2	35

WHITE SCARS

HQ	MODELS/UNIT	POINTS/MODEL**
Khan on Bike	1	110
Kor'sarro Khan	1	110

IRON HANDS

NAMED CHARACTERS	MODELS/UNIT	POINTS/MODEL**
Iron Father Feirros	1	140

IMPERIAL FISTS

NAMED CHARACTERS	MODELS/UNIT	POINTS/MODEL**
Captain Lysander	1	140
Pedro Kantor	1	155
Tor Garadon	1	145

SALAMANDERS

NAMED CHARACTERS	MODELS/UNIT	POINTS/MODEL**
Adrax Agatone	1	145
Vulkan He'stan	1	135

RAVEN GUARD

NAMED CHARACTERS	MODELS/UNIT	POINTS/MODEL**
Kayvaan Shrike	1	135

BLOOD ANGELS

HQ	MODELS/UNIT	POINTS/MODEL*
Captain	1	80
Captain in Cataphractii Armour	1	95
Captain in Gravis Armour	1	105
Captain in Phobos Armour	1	93
Captain in Terminator Armour	1	95
Captain with Jump Pack	1	105
Chaplain	1	80
Chaplain in Terminator Armour	1	95
Chaplain with Jump Pack	1	105
Librarian	1	90
Librarian Dreadnought	1	120
Librarian in Phobos Armour	1	98
Librarian in Terminator Armour	1	105
Librarian with Jump Pack	1	115
Lieutenants	1-2	65
Lieutenants in Phobos Armour	1-2	78
Lieutenants with Jump Packs	1-2	90
Primaris Captain	1	85
Primaris Chaplain	1	85
Primaris Librarian	1	95
Primaris Lieutenants	1-2	70
Sanguinary Priest	1	65
Sanguinary Priest with Jump Pack	1	90
Techmarine	1	50

NAMED CHARACTERS	MODELS/UNIT	POINTS/MODEL**
Astorath	1	110
Brother Corbulo	1	90
Captain Tycho	1	100
Chief Librarian Mephiston	1	170
Commander Dante	1	170
Gabriel Seth	1	140
Lemartes	1	110
The Sanguinor	1	140
Tycho the Lost	1	85

TROOPS	MODELS/UNIT	POINTS/MODEL*
Incursor Squad	5-10	21
Infiltrator Squad	5-10	24 [Infiltrator Helix Adept is 34]
Intercessor Squad	5-10	20
Scout Squad	5-10	14
Tactical Squad	5-10	15

ELITES	MODELS/UNIT	POINTS/MODEL*
Aggressor Squad	3-6	40
Cataphractii Terminator Squad	5-10	26
Company Ancient	1	75
Company Champion	1	40
Company Veterans	2-5	17
Contemptor Dreadnought	1	105
Death Company	5-15	19
Death Company with Jump Packs	5-15	21
Death Company Dreadnought	1	85
Death Company Intercessors	5-10	23
Dreadnought	1	70
Invictor Tactical Warsuit	1	135

ELITES	MODELS/UNIT	POINTS/MODEL**
Furioso Dreadnought	1	75
Primaris Ancient	1	80
Primaris Apothecary	1	60
Redemptor Dreadnought	1	125
Reiver Squad	5-10	18
Sanguinary Ancient	1	75
Sanguinary Guard	4-10	24
Sanguinary Novitiate	1	60
Servitors	4	7
Sternguard Veteran Squad	5-10	17
Tartaros Terminator Squad	5-10	23
Terminator Ancient	1	90
Terminator Assault Squad	5-10	23
Terminator Squad	5-10	23
Vanguard Veteran Squad	5-10	17
Vanguard Veteran Squad with Jump Packs	5-10	19

FAST ATTACK	MODELS/UNIT	POINTS/MODEL*
Assault Squad	5-10	15
Assault Squad with Jump Packs	5-10	17
Attack Bike Squad	1-3	30
Bike Squad	3-8	25
- Attack Bike	0-1	30
Inceptor Squad	3-6	40
Land Speeders	1-3	45
Scout Bike Squad	3-9	25
Suppressor Squad	3	33

HEAVY SUPPORT	MODELS/UNIT	POINTS/MODEL*
Baal Predator	1	100
Devastator Squad	5-10	15
Eliminator Squad	3	28
Hellblaster Squad	5-10	33
Hunter	1	95
Land Raider	1	175
Land Raider Crusader	1	215
Land Raider Redeemer	1	245
Predator	1	90
Repulsor Executioner	1	250
Stalker	1	95
Vindicator	1	130
Whirlwind	1	125

DEDICATED TRANSPORTS	MODELS/UNIT	POINTS/MODEL*
Drop Pod	1	65
Impulsor	1	100
Land Speeder Storm	1	40
Razorback	1	80
Repulsor	1	230
Rhino	1	75

FLYERS	MODELS/UNIT	POINTS/MODEL*
Stormhawk Interceptor	1	115
Stormraven Gunship	1	240
Stormtalon Gunship	1	105

RANGED WEAPONS	POINTS/WEAPON	RANGED WEAPONS	POINTS/WEAPON
Absolvor bolt pistol	0	Master-crafted occulus bolt carbine	0
Accelerator autocannon	0	Master-crafted stalker bolt rifle	5
Angelus boltgun	0	Melta bombs	5
Assault bolter	0	Meltagun	10
Assault cannon (INFANTRY/other model)	15/20	Missile launcher (INFANTRY/other model)	15/20
Assault plasma incinerator	0	Multi-melta (INFANTRY/other model)	20/25
Astartes grenade launcher	0	Occulus bolt carbine	0
Astartes shotgun	0	Onslaught gatling cannon	20
Auto bolt rifle	0	Plasma blaster	10
Auto boltstorm gauntlets	0	Plasma cannon	10
Bellicatus missile array	20	Plasma cutter	5
Bolt carbine	0	Plasma exterminator	5
Bolt pistol	0	Plasma gun	10
Bolt rifle	0	Plasma incinerator	0
Bolt sniper rifle	0	Plasma pistol	5
Boltgun	0	Predator autocannon	40
Boltstorm gauntlet	0	Reaper autocannon	10
Cerberus launcher	0	Reductor pistol	0
Combi-bolter	3	Shock grenades	0
Combi-flamer	10	Skyhammer missile launcher	20
Combi-grav	10	Skyspear missile launcher	0
Combi-melta	10	Sniper rifle	2
Combi-plasma	10	Special issue boltgun	0
Cyclone missile launcher	25	Stalker bolt rifle	0
Deathwind launcher	5	Storm bolter	3
Demolisher cannon	0	Stormstrike missile launcher	0
Flamer	5	Twin assault cannon	40
Flamestorm cannon (Baal Predator)	25	Twin boltgun	0
Flamestorm cannon (other model)	0	Twin heavy bolter	30
Flamestorm gauntlets	0	Twin heavy plasma cannon	40
Frag cannon	20	Twin Icarus ironhail heavy stubber	0
Frag grenades	0	Twin ironhail autocannon	0
Fragstorm grenade launcher	5	Twin lascannon	40
Grav-cannon and grav-amp (INFANTRY/other model)	10/15	Twin multi-melta	50
Grav-gun	10	Typhoon missile launcher	40
Grav-pistol	5	Volkite charger	5
Grenade harness	5	Whirlwind castellan launcher	0
Hand flamer	5	Whirlwind vengeance launcher	10
Heavy bolt pistol	0	Wrist-mounted grenade launcher	5
Heavy bolter (INFANTRY/other model)	10/15		
Heavy flamer (INFANTRY/other model)	10/15		

Heavy laser destroyer	40	MELEE WEAPONS	POINTS/WEAPON
Heavy onslaught gatling cannon	30	Blood talons	35
Heavy plasma cannon	20	Chainfist	10
Heavy plasma incinerator	0	Chainsword	0
Hunter-killer missile	5	Combat knife	0
Hurricane bolter	15	Crozius arcanum	0
Icarus ironhail heavy stubber	5	Dreadnought combat weapon	20
Icarus rocket pod	5	Encarmine axe	10
Icarus stormcannon	10	Encarmine sword	10
Incendium cannon	0	Eviscerator	10
Inferno pistol	5	Force axe	0
Ironhail heavy stubber	5	Force stave	0
Kheres pattern assault cannon	25	Force sword	0
Krak grenades	0	Furioso fist (single/pair)	20/30
Krakstorm grenade launcher	5	Furioso force halberd	0
Las-talon	35	Invictor fist	0
Lascannon (INFANTRY/other model)	15/20	Lightning claws (single/pair)	5/10
Macro plasma incinerator	30	Master-crafted power sword	10
Marksman bolt carbine	0	Paired combat blades	0
Master-crafted auto bolt rifle	5	Power axe	5
Master-crafted boltgun	5	Power fist	10
Master-crafted instigator bolt carbine	0	Power maul	5

MELEE WEAPONS	POINTS/WEAPON
Power sword	5
Redemptor fist	0
Relic blade	10
Servo-arm	0
Thunder hammer (CHARACTER/other model)	40/15

OTHER WARGEAR	POINTS/ITEM
Armorium cherub	5
Auto launchers	0
Auxiliary grenade launcher	2
Camo cloak	2

OTHER WARGEAR	POINTS/ITEM
Combat shield	3
Death mask	0
Grapnel launcher	2
Grav-chute	2
Haywire mine	10
Magna-grapple	5
Orbital comms array	20
Shield dome	25
Smoke grenades	0
Storm shield (CHARACTER/other model)	10/4
Teleport homer	5

DARK ANGELS

HQ	MODELS/UNIT	POINTS/MODEL*
Chaplain	1	80
Chaplain with Jump Pack	1	105
Interrogator-Chaplain	1	85
Interrogator-Chaplain in Terminator Armour	1	105
Interrogator-Chaplain with Jump Pack	1	110
Librarian	1	90
Librarian in Phobos Armour	1	98
Librarian in Terminator Armour	1	105
Librarian with Jump Pack	1	115
Lieutenants	1-2	65
Lieutenants with Jump Packs	1-2	90
Lieutenants in Phobos Armour	1-2	78
Master	1	80
Master in Cataphractii Armour	1	95
Master in Gravis Armour	1	105
Master in Phobos Armour	1	93
Master in Terminator Armour	1	95
Master with Jump Pack	1	105
Primaris Chaplain	1	85
Primaris Librarian	1	95
Primaris Lieutenants	1-2	70
Primaris Master	1	85
Ravenwing Talonmaster	1	105
Techmarine	1	50

NAMED CHARACTERS	MODELS/UNIT	POINTS/MODEL**
Asmodai	1	115
Azrael	1	160
Belial	1	125
Ezekiel	1	115
Lazarus	1	110
Sammael in Sableclaw	1	210
Sammael on Corvex	1	140

TROOPS	MODELS/UNIT	POINTS/MODEL*
Incursor Squad	5-10	21
Infiltrator Squad	5-10	24 (Infiltrator Helix Adept is 34)
Intercessor Squad	5-10	20
Scout Squad	5-10	14
Tactical Squad	5-10	15

ELITES	MODELS/UNIT	POINTS/MODEL*
Aggressor Squad	3-6	40
Apothecary	1	55
Chapter Ancient	1	95
Company Ancient	1	75
Company Champion	1	40
Company Veterans	2-5	17
Contemptor Dreadnought	1	105
Deathwing Ancient	1	75
Deathwing Apothecary	1	75
Deathwing Cataphractii Terminator Squad	5-10	26
Deathwing Champion	1	95
Deathwing Knights	5-10	41
Deathwing Terminator Squad	5-10	23
Deathwing Tartaros Terminator Squad	5-10	23
Dreadnought	1	70
Invictor Tactical Warsuit	1	135
Primaris Ancient	1	80
Primaris Apothecary	1	60
Ravenwing Ancient	1	85
Ravenwing Apothecary	1	65
Ravenwing Champion	1	80
Redemptor Dreadnought	1	125
Reiver Squad	5-10	18
Servitors	4	7
Venerable Dreadnought	1	85

FAST ATTACK	MODELS/UNIT	POINTS/MODEL*
Assault Squad	5-10	15
Assault Squad with Jump Packs	5-10	17
Inceptor Squad	3-6	40
Ravenwing Attack Bike Squad	1-3	30
Ravenwing Bike Squad	3-8	25
- Ravenwing Attack Bike	0-1	30
Ravenwing Black Knights	3-10	40
Ravenwing Darkshroud	1	120
Ravenwing Land Speeders	1-5	45
Ravenwing Land Speeder Vengeance	1	105
Scout Bike Squad	3-9	25
Suppressor Squad	3	33

HEAVY SUPPORT	MODELS/UNIT	POINTS/MODEL*
Devastator Squad	5-10	15
Eliminator Squad	3	28
Hellblaster Squad	5-10	33
Hunter	1	95
Land Raider	1	175
Land Raider Crusader	1	215
Land Raider Redeemer	1	245
Predator	1	90
Repulsor Executioner	1	250
Stalker	1	95
Vindicator	1	130
Whirlwind	1	125

DEDICATED TRANSPORTS	MODELS/UNIT	POINTS/MODEL*
Drop Pod	1	65
Impulsor	1	100
Land Speeder Storm	1	40
Razorback	1	80
Repulsor	1	230
Rhino	1	75

FLYERS	MODELS/UNIT	POINTS/MODEL*
Nephilim Jetfighter	1	105
Ravenwing Dark Talon	1	185
Stormraven Gunship	1	240

RANGED WEAPONS	POINTS/WEAPON
Absolvor bolt pistol	0
Accelerator autocannon	0
Assault bolter	0
Assault cannon (INFANTRY/other model)	15/20
Assault plasma incinerator	0
Astartes grenade launcher	0
Astartes shotgun	0
Auto boltstorm gauntlets	0
Auto bolt rifle	0
Avenger mega bolter	35
Bellicatus missile array	20
Blacksword missile launcher	0
Bolt carbine	0
Bolt carbine with special issue ammunition	5
Bolt pistol	0
Bolt rifle	0
Bolt sniper rifle	0
Boltgun	0
Boltstorm gauntlet	0
Cerberus launcher	0
Combi-bolter	3
Combi-flamer	10
Combi-grav	10
Combi-melta	10
Combi-plasma	10
Cyclone missile launcher	25
Deathwind launcher	5
Demolisher cannon	0
Flamer	5
Flamestorm cannon	0
Flamestorm gauntlets	0
Frag grenades	0
Fragstorm grenade launcher	5

RANGED WEAPONS	POINTS/WEAPON
Grav-pistol	5
Grav-cannon and grav-amp (INFANTRY/other model)	10/15
Grav-gun	10
Grenade harness	5
Heavy bolter (INFANTRY/other model)	10/15
Heavy bolt pistol	0
Heavy flamer (INFANTRY/other model)	10/15
Heavy laser destroyer	40
Heavy onslaught gatling cannon	30
Heavy plasma cannon	20
Heavy plasma incinerator	0
Hunter-killer missile	5
Hurricane bolter	15
Icarus ironhail heavy stubber	5
Icarus rocket pod	5
Icarus stormcannon	10
Ironhail heavy stubber	5
Kheres pattern assault cannon	25
Krak grenades	0
Krakstorm grenade launcher	5
Lascannon (INFANTRY/other model)	15/20
Las-talon	35
Macro plasma incinerator	30
Marksman bolt carbine	0
Master-crafted auto bolt rifle	5
Master-crafted boltgun	5
Master-crafted instigator bolt carbine	0
Master-crafted occulus bolt carbine	0
Master-crafted stalker bolt rifle	5
Melta bombs	5
Meltagun	10
Missile launcher (INFANTRY/other model)	15/20
Multi-melta (INFANTRY/other model)	20/20
Occulus bolt carbine	0
Onslaught gatling cannon	20
Plasma blaster	10
Plasma cannon	10
Plasma cutter	5
Plasma exterminator	5
Plasma gun	10
Plasma incinerator	0
Plasma pistol	5
Plasma storm battery	0
Plasma talon	0
Predator autocannon	40
Ravenwing grenade launcher	0
Reaper autocannon	10
Reductor pistol	0
Rift cannon	0
Shock grenades	0
Skyspear missile launcher	0
Sniper rifle	2
Stalker bolt rifle	0
Storm bolter	3
Stormstrike missile launcher	0
Twin assault cannon	40
Twin boltgun	0
Twin heavy bolter	30
Twin heavy plasma cannon	40
Twin Icarus ironhail heavy stubber	0
Twin ironhail autocannon	0
Twin lascannon	40
Twin multi-melta	50

RANGED WEAPONS	POINTS/WEAPON
Typhoon missile launcher	40
Volkite charger	5
Whirlwind castellan launcher	0
Whirlwind vengeance launcher	10
Wrist-mounted grenade launcher	5

MELEE WEAPONS	POINTS/WEAPON
Blade of Caliban	0
Chainfist	10
Chainsword	0
Combat knife	0
Corvus hammer	0
Crozius arcanum	0
Dreadnought combat weapon	20
Eviscerator	10
Flail of the Unforgiven	0
Force axe	0
Force stave	0
Force sword	0
Halberd of Caliban	0
Invictor fist	0
Lightning claws (single/pair)	5/10
Mace of absolution	0
Master-crafted power sword	10

MELEE WEAPONS	POINTS/WEAPON
Paired combat blades	0
Power axe	5
Power fist	10
Power maul	5
Power sword	5
Redemptor fist	0
Relic blade	10
Servo-arm	0
Thunder hammer (CHARACTER/other model)	40/15

OTHER WARGEAR	POINTS/ITEM
Armorium Cherub	5
Auto launchers	0
Auxiliary grenade launcher	2
Camo cloak	2
Combat shield	3
Grapnel launcher	2
Grav-chute	2
Haywire mine	10
Orbital comms array	20
Shield dome	25
Smoke grenades	0
Storm shield (CHARACTER/other model)	10/4
Watcher in the Dark	5

SPACE WOLVES

HQ	MODELS/UNIT	POINTS/MODEL*
Bjorn the Fell-Handed	1	155
Iron Priest	1	50
Primaris Battle Leader	1	70
Primaris Battle Leaders in Phobos Armour	1-2	78
Primaris Rune Priest	1	95
Primaris Wolf Lord	1	90
Primaris Wolf Priest	1	85
Rune Priest	1	90
Rune Priest in Phobos Armour	1	98
Rune Priest in Terminator Armour	1	105
Rune Priest with Jump Pack	1	115
Wolf Guard Battle Leader	1	65
Wolf Guard Battle Leader in Terminator Armour	1	80
Wolf Guard Battle Leader on Thunderwolf	1	90
Wolf Guard Battle Leader with Jump Pack	1	90
Wolf Lord	1	85
Wolf Lord in Cataphractii Armour	1	95
Wolf Lord in Gravis Armour	1	105
Wolf Lord in Phobos Armour	1	93
Wolf Lord in Terminator Armour	1	95
Wolf Lord on Thunderwolf	1	100
Wolf Lord with Jump Pack	1	105
Wolf Priest	1	80
Wolf Priest in Terminator Armour	1	95
Wolf Priest with Jump Pack	1	105

NAMED CHARACTERS	MODELS/UNIT	POINTS/MODEL**
Arjac Rockfist	1	115
Canis Wolfborn	1	110
Harald Deathwolf	1	145
Krom Dragongaze	1	90
Logan Grimnar	1	150
Logan Grimnar on Stormrider	1	165
Lukas the Trickster	1	85
Murderfang	1	135
Njal Stormcaller	1	125
Njal Stormcaller in Runic Terminator Armour	1	140
Ragnar Blackmane	1	125
Ulrik the Slayer	1	100

TROOPS	MODELS/UNIT	POINTS/MODEL*
Blood Claws	5-15	15
Grey Hunters	5-10	15
Incursors	5-10	21
Infiltrators	5-10	24 (Infiltrator Helix Adept is 34)
Intercessors	5-10	20
Wolf Guard Pack Leader	-	17
Wolf Guard Terminator Pack Leader	-	23

ELITES	MODELS/UNIT	POINTS/MODEL*
Aggressors	3-6	40
Contemptor Dreadnought	1	105
Dreadnought	1	70
Great Company Ancient	1	75
Great Company Champion	1	40
Invictor Tactical Warsuit	1	135
Primaris Ancient	1	80
Redemptor Dreadnought	1	125
Reivers	5-10	18
Servitors	4	7
Venerable Dreadnought	1	85
Wolf Guard	5-10	17
Wolf Guard Cataphractii Terminators	5-10	26
Wolf Guard Pack Leader	-	19
Wolf Guard Tartaros Terminators	5-10	23
Wolf Guard Terminators	5-10	23
Wolf Guard Terminator Pack Leader	-	23
Wolf Guard with Jump Packs	5-10	19
Wolf Scouts	5-10	14
Wulfen	5-10	28
Wulfen Dreadnought	1	75

FAST ATTACK	MODELS/UNIT	POINTS/MODEL*
Cyberwolves	1-5	15
Fenrisian Wolves	5-15	7 (Cyberwolf is 15)
Inceptors	3-6	25
Land Speeders	1-3	45
Skyclaws	5-15	18
Suppressors	3	18
Swiftclaw Attack Bikes	1-3	30
Swiftclaws	3-15	25
- Swiftclaw Attack Bike	0-1	30
Thunderwolf Cavalry	3-6	45
Wolf Guard Bike Leader	-	30
Wolf Guard Sky Leader	-	20
Wolf Scout Bikers	3-9	25

HEAVY SUPPORT	MODELS/UNIT	POINTS/MODEL*
Eliminators	3	28
Hellblasters	5-10	33
Hunter	1	95
Land Raider	1	175
Land Raider Crusader	1	215
Land Raider Redeemer	1	245
Long Fangs	5-6	16
Predator	1	90
Repulsor Executioner	1	250
Stalker	1	95
Vindicator	1	130
Whirlwind	1	125
Wolf Guard Pack Leader	-	17
Wolf Guard Terminator Pack Leader	-	23

DEDICATED TRANSPORT	MODELS/UNIT	POINTS/MODEL*
Drop Pod	1	65
Impulsor	1	100
Land Speeder Storm	1	40
Razorback	1	80
Repulsor	1	230
Rhino	1	75

FLYERS	MODELS/UNIT	POINTS/MODEL*
Stormfang Gunship	1	180
Stormhawk Interceptor	1	115
Stormwolf	1	170

RANGED WEAPONS	POINTS/WEAPON
Absolvor bolt pistol	0
Accelerator autocannon	0
Assault bolter	0
Assault cannon (INFANTRY/other model)	15/20
Assault plasma incinerator	0
Astartes grenade launcher	0
Astartes shotgun	0
Auto bolt rifle	0
Auto boltstorm gauntlets	0
Bellicatus missile array	20
Bolt carbine	0
Bolt pistol	0
Bolt rifle	0
Bolt sniper rifle	0
Boltgun	0
Boltstorm gauntlet	0
Cerberus launcher	0
Combi-bolter	3
Combi-flamer	10
Combi-melta	10
Combi-plasma	10
Cyclone missile launcher	25
Deathwind launcher	5
Demolisher cannon	0
Flamer	5
Flamestorm cannon	0
Flamestorm gauntlets	0
Frag grenades	0
Fragstorm grenade launcher	5
Grenade harness	0
Heavy bolt pistol	0
Heavy bolter (INFANTRY/other model)	10/15
Heavy flamer (INFANTRY/other model)	10/15
Heavy laser destroyer	40
Heavy onslaught gatling cannon	30
Heavy plasma cannon	20
Heavy plasma incinerator	0
Helfrost cannon	20
Helfrost destructor	0
Helfrost pistol	5
Hunter-killer missile	5
Hurricane bolter	15
Icarus ironhail heavy stubber	5
Icarus rocket pod	5
Icarus stormcannon	10
Ironhail heavy stubber	5
Kheres pattern assault cannon	25
Krak grenades	0

RANGED WEAPONS	POINTS/WEAPON
Krakstorm grenade launcher	5
Las-talon	35
Lascannon (INFANTRY/other model)	15/20
Macro plasma incinerator	30
Marksman bolt carbine	0
Master-crafted auto bolt rifle	5
Master-crafted boltgun	5
Master-crafted instigator bolt carbine	0
Master-crafted occulus bolt carbine	0
Master-crafted stalker bolt rifle	5
Meltagun	10
Missile launcher (INFANTRY/other model)	15/20
Multi-melta (INFANTRY/other model)	20/25
Occulus bolt carbine	0
Onslaught gatling cannon	20
Plasma blaster	10
Plasma cannon	10
Plasma exterminator	5
Plasma gun	10
Plasma incinerator	0
Plasma pistol	5
Predator autocannon	40
Reaper autocannon	10
Shock grenades	0
Skyhammer missile launcher	20
Skyspear missile launcher	0
Sniper rifle	2
Stalker bolt rifle	0
Storm bolter	3
Stormfrag auto-launcher	4
Stormstrike missile launcher	0
Twin assault cannon	30
Twin boltgun	0
Twin heavy bolter	30
Twin helfrost cannon	40
Twin Icarus ironhail heavy stubber	0
Twin ironhail autocannon	30
Twin lascannon	40
Twin multi-melta	50
Typhoon missile launcher	40
Volkite charger	5
Whirlwind castellan launcher	0
Whirlwind vengeance launcher	10
Wrist-mounted grenade launcher	5

MELEE WEAPONS	POINTS/WEAPON
Chainfist	10
Chainsword	0
Combat knife	0
Crozius arcanum	0
Crushing teeth and claws	0
Dreadnought combat weapon	20
Fenrisian great axe	30
Frost axe	10
Frost claws	10
Frost sword	10
Great frost axe	10
Great wolf claw	20
Invictor fist	0
Lightning claws (single/pair)	5/10
Master-crafted power sword	10
Paired combat blades	0
Power axe	5
Power fist	10
Power maul	5
Power sword	5
Redemptor fist	0
Runic axe	0
Runic stave	0
Runic sword	0
Servo-arm	0
Teeth and claws	0
Tempest hammer	20
Thunder hammer (CHARACTER/other model)	40/15
Trueclaw	0
Wolf claw (single/pair)	7/15
Wulfen claws	0

OTHER WARGEAR	POINTS/ITEM
Auto launchers	0
Auxiliary grenade launcher	2
Blizzard shield	15
Camo cloak	2
Combat shield	3
Grapnel launcher	2
Grav-chute	2
Haywire mine	10
Orbital comms array	20
Psychic hood	5
Runic armour	10
Runic Terminator armour	5
Shield dome	25
Smoke grenades	0
Storm shield (CHARACTER)	10
Storm shield (Thunderwolf Cavalry)	8
Storm shield (other model)	4
Teleport homer	5
Wolf standard	10

DEATHWATCH

HQ	MODELS/UNIT	POINTS/MODEL*
Chaplain	1	80
Chaplain in Terminator Armour	1	95
Chaplain with Jump Pack	1	105
Librarian	1	90
Librarian in Terminator Armour	1	105
Librarian with Jump Pack	1	115
Primaris Chaplain	1	85
Primaris Librarian	1	95
Primaris Watch Captain	1	85
Watch Captain	1	80
Watch Captain in Terminator Armour	1	95
Watch Captain with Jump Pack	1	105
Watch Master	1	125

NAMED CHARACTERS	MODELS/UNIT	POINTS/MODEL**
Watch Captain Artemis	1	110

TROOPS	MODELS/UNIT	POINTS/MODEL*
Intercessors	5-10	20
- Aggressors	-	40
- Hellblasters	-	33
- Inceptors	-	40
- Reivers	-	18
Veterans	5-10	17
- Bikers	-	28
- Black Shield	-	19
- Terminators	-	23
- Vanguard Veterans	-	19

ELITES	MODELS/UNIT	POINTS/MODEL*
Aggressors	3-6	40
Dreadnought	1	70
Primaris Apothecary	1	60
Redemptor Dreadnought	1	125
Reivers	5-10	18
Terminators	5-10	23
Vanguard Veterans	5-10	19
Venerable Dreadnought	1	85

FAST ATTACK	MODELS/UNIT	POINTS/MODEL*
Bikers	3-6	28
Inceptors	3-6	40

HEAVY SUPPORT	MODELS/UNIT	POINTS/MODEL*
Hellblasters	5-10	33
Land Raider	1	175
Land Raider Crusader	1	215
Land Raider Redeemer	1	245
Repulsor Executioner	1	250

FLYERS	MODELS/UNIT	POINTS/MODEL*
Corvus Blackstar	1	140

DEDICATED TRANSPORT	MODELS/UNIT	POINTS/MODEL*
Drop Pod	1	65
Razorback	1	80
Repulsor	1	230
Rhino	1	75

RANGED WEAPONS	POINTS/WEAPON
Absolvor bolt pistol	0
Assault bolter	0
Assault cannon (INFANTRY/other model)	15/20
Assault plasma incinerator	0
Auto bolt rifle	0
Auto boltstorm gauntlets	0
Blackstar rocket launcher	0
Bolt carbine	0
Bolt pistol	0
Bolt rifle	0
Boltgun	0
Combi-flamer	10
Combi-grav	10
Combi-melta	10
Combi-plasma	10
Cyclone missile launcher	25
Deathwatch frag cannon	20
Deathwatch shotgun	2
Deathwind launcher	5
Flamer	5
Flamestorm cannon	0
Flamestorm gauntlets	0
Frag grenades	0
Fragstorm grenade launcher	5
Grav-gun	10
Grav-pistol	5
Hand flamer	5
Heavy bolt pistol	0
Heavy bolter (INFANTRY/other model)	10/15
Heavy flamer (INFANTRY/other model)	10/15
Heavy laser destroyer	40
Heavy onslaught gatling cannon	30
Heavy plasma cannon	20
Heavy plasma incinerator	0
Hunter-killer missile	5
Hurricane bolter	15
Icarus ironhail heavy stubber	5
Icarus rocket pod	5
Inferno pistol	5
Infernus heavy bolter	20
Ironhail heavy stubber	5
Krak grenades	0
Krakstorm grenade launcher	5
Las-talon	35
Macro plasma incinerator	30
Master-crafted auto bolt rifle	5
Master-crafted boltgun	5
Master-crafted stalker bolt rifle	5
Melta bombs	5
Meltagun	10
Missile launcher (INFANTRY/other model)	15/20
Multi-melta	25
Onslaught gatling cannon	20

* Excluding wargear
** Including wargear

RANGED WEAPONS	POINTS/WEAPON
Plasma exterminator	5
Plasma gun	10
Plasma incinerator	0
Plasma pistol	5
Reductor pistol	0
Shock grenades	0
Stalker bolt rifle	0
Stalker pattern boltgun	2
Storm bolter	3
Stormstrike missile launcher	0
Twin assault cannon	40
Twin boltgun	0
Twin heavy bolter	30
Twin Icarus ironhail heavy stubber	0
Twin lascannon	40

MELEE WEAPONS	POINTS/WEAPON
Force sword	0
Guardian spear	0
Heavy thunder hammer	20
Lightning claws (single/pair)	5/10
Power axe	5
Power fist	10
Power maul	5
Power sword	5
Redemptor fist	0
Relic blade	10
Thunder hammer (CHARACTER/other model)	40/15
Xenophase blade	10

MELEE WEAPONS	POINTS/WEAPON
Chainfist	10
Chainsword	0
Combat knife	0
Crozius arcanum	0
Dreadnought combat weapon	20
Force axe	0
Force stave	0

OTHER WARGEAR	POINTS/ITEM
Auspex array	5
Auto launchers	0
Auxiliary grenade launcher	2
Blackstar cluster launcher	0
Combat shield	3
Deathwatch teleport homer	5
Grapnel launcher	2
Grav-chute	2
Infernum halo-launcher	5
Storm shield (CHARACTER/other model)	10/4

GREY KNIGHTS

HQ	MODELS/UNIT	POINTS/MODEL*
Brother-Captain	1	115
Brotherhood Champion	1	90
Chaplain	1	110
Grand Master	1	135
Grand Master in Nemesis Dreadknight	1	180
Librarian	1	105
Techmarine	1	60

NAMED CHARACTERS	MODELS/UNIT	POINTS/MODEL**
Brother-Captain Stern	1	110
Castellan Crowe	1	85
Grand Master Voldus	1	160
Lord Kaldor Draigo	1	190

TROOPS	MODELS/UNIT	POINTS/MODEL*
Strike Squad	5-10	17
Terminator Squad	5-10	35

DEDICATED TRANSPORT	MODELS/UNIT	POINTS/MODEL*
Razorback	1	80
Rhino	1	75

ELITES	MODELS/UNIT	POINTS/MODEL*
Apothecary	1	80
Brotherhood Ancient	1	100
Brotherhood Champion	1	95
Dreadnought	1	80
Paladin Ancient	1	100
Paladin Squad	3-10	47
Purifier Squad	5-10	17
Servitors	4	7
Venerable Dreadnought	1	95

FAST ATTACK	MODELS/UNIT	POINTS/MODEL*
Interceptor Squad	5-10	20

HEAVY SUPPORT	MODELS/UNIT	POINTS/MODEL*
Land Raider	1	175
Land Raider Crusader	1	215
Land Raider Redeemer	1	245
Nemesis Dreadknight	1	130
Purgation Squad	5-10	17

FLYERS	MODELS/UNIT	POINTS/MODEL*
Stormhawk Interceptor	1	115
Stormraven Gunship	1	240
Stormtalon Gunship	1	105

RANGED WEAPONS	POINTS/WEAPON
Assault cannon	20
Bolt pistol	0
Boltgun	0
Combi-flamer	10
Combi-melta	10
Combi-plasma	10
Flamer	5
Flamestorm cannon	0
Frag grenades	0
Gatling psilencer	20
Heavy bolter (INFANTRY/other model)	10/15
Heavy flamer	15
Heavy incinerator	20
Heavy plasma cannon	20
Heavy psycannon	25
Hunter-killer missile	5
Hurricane bolter	15
Icarus stormcannon	10
Incinerator	15
Krak grenades	0
Las-talon	35
Lascannon	20
Missile launcher	20
Multi-melta (INFANTRY/other model)	20/25
Plasma cannon	15
Plasma cutter	5
Psilencer	5
Psycannon	10

RANGED WEAPONS	POINTS/WEAPON
Psyk-out grenades	0
Skyhammer missile launcher	20
Storm bolter	3
Stormstrike missile launcher	0
Twin assault cannon	40
Twin heavy bolter	30
Twin heavy plasma cannon	40
Twin lascannon	40
Twin multi-melta	50
Typhoon missile launcher	40

MELEE WEAPONS	POINTS/WEAPON
Crozius arcanum	0
Dreadfist/two Dreadfists	0/5
Dreadnought combat weapon	20
Nemesis Daemon greathammer	15
Nemesis Daemon hammer	15
Nemesis falchion	2
Nemesis force halberd	0
Nemesis force sword	0
Nemesis greatsword	10
Nemesis warding stave	0
Power axe	5
Servo-arm	0

OTHER WARGEAR	POINTS/ITEM
Dreadknight teleporter	10

FORCES OF THE IMPERIUM

ADEPTA SORORITAS

HQ	MODELS/UNIT	POINTS/MODEL*
Canoness	1	50
Missionary	1	45

NAMED CHARACTERS	MODELS/UNIT	POINTS/MODEL**
Junith Eruita	1	115
Celestine	1	170
Geminae Superia	1-2	18
Triumph of Saint Katherine	1	195

TROOPS	MODELS/UNIT	POINTS/MODEL*
Battle Sisters Squad	5-15	11

ELITES	MODELS/UNIT	POINTS/MODEL*
Arco-flagellants	3-10	15
Celestian Squad	5-10	12
Crusaders	2-6	11
Death Cult Assassins	2-6	13
Dialogus	1	40
Hospitaller	1	40

ELITES	MODELS/UNIT	POINTS/MODEL*
Imagifier	1	45
Preacher	1	35
Repentia Superior	1	40
Sisters Repentia	4-9	15
Zephyrim Squad	5-10	15

FAST ATTACK	MODELS/UNIT	POINTS/MODEL*
Dominion Squad	5-10	12
Seraphim Squad	5-10	15

HEAVY SUPPORT	MODELS/UNIT	POINTS/MODEL*
Exorcist	1	150
Mortifiers	1-4	30
- Anchorite		35
Penitent Engines	1-4	20
Retributor Squad	5-10	12

DEDICATED TRANSPORT

DEDICATED TRANSPORT	MODELS/UNIT	POINTS/MODEL*
Immolator	1	80
Sororitas Rhino	1	75

FORTIFICATION	MODELS/UNIT	POINTS/MODEL**
Battle Sanctum	1	55

RANGED WEAPONS	POINTS/WEAPON
Autogun	0
Bolt pistol	0
Boltgun	0
Combi-flamer	10
Combi-melta	10
Combi-plasma	10
Condemnor boltgun	5
Exorcist conflagration rockets	0
Exorcist missile launcher	30
Flamer	5
Frag grenades	0
Hand flamer (SERAPHIM/other model)	2/5
Heavy bolter (INFANTRY/other model)	10/15
Heavy flamer (INFANTRY/other model)	10/15
Hunter-killer missile	5
Immolation flamers	30
Inferno pistol	5
Krak grenades	0
Laspistol	0
Meltagun	10
Multi-melta (INFANTRY/other model)	20/25
Plasma pistol	5
Shotgun	0
Storm bolter	3
Twin heavy bolter	30
Twin multi-melta	50

MELEE WEAPONS	POINTS/WEAPON
Arco-flails	0
Blessed blade	10
Chainsword	0
Chirurgeon's tools	0
Death Cult power blades	0
Dialogus staff	0
Neural whips	0
Penitent buzz-blade	0
Penitent eviscerator	0
Penitent flail	0
Power maul	5
Power sword	5

OTHER WARGEAR	POINTS/ITEM
Armorium cherub	5
Brazier of holy fire	10
Incensor Cherub	5
Null rod	10
Rod of office	5
Simulacrum Imperialis	5
Storm shield	0
Zephyrim pennant	5

ADEPTUS CUSTODES

HQ	MODELS/UNIT	POINTS/MODEL*
Shield-Captain	1	95
Shield-Captain in Allarus Terminator Armour	1	105
Shield-Captain on Dawneagle Jetbike	1	175

NAMED CHARACTERS	MODELS/UNIT	POINTS/MODEL**
Captain-General Trajann Valoris	1	190

TROOPS	MODELS/UNIT	POINTS/MODEL*
Custodian Guard	3-10	44

ELITES	MODELS/UNIT	POINTS/MODEL*
Allarus Custodians	3-10	60
Custodian Wardens	3-10	47
Venerable Contemptor Dreadnought	1	130
Vexilus Praetor	1	85
Vexilus Praetor in Allarus Terminator Armour	1	95

FAST ATTACK	MODELS/UNIT	POINTS/MODEL*
Vertus Praetors	3-10	95

HEAVY SUPPORT	MODELS/UNIT	POINTS/MODEL*
Venerable Land Raider	1	300

RANGED WEAPONS	POINTS/WEAPON
Balistus grenade launcher	0
Castellan axe	10
Combi-bolter	0
Guardian spear	5
Hunter-killer missile	5
Hurricane bolter	0
Kheres-pattern assault cannon	25
Multi-melta	25
Salvo launcher	0
Sentinel blade	7
Storm bolter	3
Twin heavy bolter	0
Twin lascannon	0

MELEE WEAPONS	POINTS/WEAPON
Dreadnought combat weapon	0
Interceptor lance	0
Misericordia	3

OTHER WARGEAR	POINTS/ITEM
Storm shield (CHARACTER/other model)	10/5
Vexilla Defensor	20
Vexilla Imperius	20
Vexilla Magnifica	30

SISTERS OF SILENCE

ELITES	MODELS/UNIT	POINTS/MODEL*
Prosecutors	5-10	12
Vigilators	5-10	17
Witchseekers	5-10	18

DEDICATED TRANSPORT	MODELS/UNIT	POINTS/MODEL*
Null-Maiden Rhino	1	75

RANGED WEAPONS	POINTS/WEAPON
Boltgun	0
Flamer	0
Hunter-killer missile	5
Psyk-out grenades	0
Storm bolter	0

MELEE WEAPONS	POINTS/WEAPON
Executioner greatblade	0

OFFICIO ASSASSINORUM

ELITES	MODELS/UNIT	POINTS/MODEL**
Callidus Assassin	1	100
Culexus Assassin	1	100
Eversor Assassin	1	100
Vindicare Assassin	1	100

ASTRA MILITARUM

HQ	MODELS/UNIT	POINTS/MODEL*
Company Commander	1	35
Knight Commander Pask	1	185
Lord Commissar	1	35
Primaris Psyker	1	50
Tank Commander	1	155
Tempestor Prime	1	40

NAMED CHARACTERS	MODELS/UNIT	POINTS/MODEL**
Colonel 'Iron Hand' Straken	1	80
Colour Sergeant Kell	1	45
Commissar Yarrick	1	105
Lord Castellan Creed	1	60
Nork Deddog	1	60
Sergeant Harker	1	55
Severina Raine	1	35
Sly Marbo	1	60

TROOPS	MODELS/UNIT	POINTS/MODEL*
Conscripts	20-30	5
Infantry Squad†	10	5
Militarum Tempestus Scions	5-10	9

ELITES	MODELS/UNIT	POINTS/MODEL*
Astropath	1	25
Bullgryns	3-9	38
Command Squad†	4	6
Commissar	1	20
Crusaders	2-10	15
Master of Ordnance	1	35
Militarum Tempestus Command Squad	4	10

ELITES	MODELS/UNIT	POINTS/MODEL*
Ministorum Priest	1	40
Officer of the Fleet	1	25
Ogryn Bodyguard	1	50
Ogryns	3-9	30
Platoon Commander	1	25
Ratlings	5-10	8
Servitors	4	7
Special Weapons Squad	6	5
Tech-Priest Enginseer	1	35
Veterans†	10	6
Wyrdvane Psykers	3-9	8

FAST ATTACK	MODELS/UNIT	POINTS/MODEL*
Armoured Sentinels	1-3	30
Hellhounds	1-3	95
Scout Sentinels	1-3	30

HEAVY SUPPORT	MODELS/UNIT	POINTS/MODEL*
Basilisks	1-3	110
Deathstrike	1	135
Heavy Weapons Squad	3	7
Hydras	1-3	95
Leman Russ Battle Tanks	1-3	130
Manticore	1	130
Wyverns	1-3	120

DEDICATED TRANSPORT	MODELS/UNIT	POINTS/MODEL*
Chimera	1	65
Taurox	1	60
Taurox Prime	1	90

* Excluding wargear
** Including wargear
† If models in these units form Heavy Weapons Teams, there is no
  additional points cost.

FLYER	MODELS/UNIT	POINTS/MODEL*
Valkyries	1-3	105

LORDS OF WAR	MODELS/UNIT	POINTS/MODEL*
Baneblade	1	385
Banehammer	1	380
Banesword	1	380
Doomhammer	1	390
Hellhammer	1	425
Shadowsword	1	440
Stormlord	1	430
Stormsword	1	410

RANGED WEAPONS	POINTS/WEAPON
Artillery barrage	0
Autocannon (INFANTRY/other model)	10/15
Autogun	0
Baneblade cannon	0
Battle cannon	20
Bolt pistol (COMMISSAR/other model)	0/2
Boltgun	2
Chem cannon	0
Deathstrike missile	0
Demolisher cannon	20
Earthshaker cannon	0
Eradicator nova cannon	15
Executioner plasma cannon	15
Exterminator autocannon	30
Flamer	5
Frag bomb	0
Frag grenades	0
Grenade launcher	5
Grenadier gauntlet	5
Heavy bolter (INFANTRY/other model)	10/15
Heavy flamer (INFANTRY/other model)	10/15
Heavy stubber	5
Hellhammer cannon	0
Hellstrike missiles	10
Hot-shot lasgun	0
Hot-shot laspistol	0
Hot-shot volley gun	5
Hunter-killer missile	5
Hydra quad autocannon	0
Inferno cannon	10
Krak grenades	0
Lascannon (INFANTRY/other model)	15/20
Lasgun	0
Lasgun array	0
Laspistol	0
Magma cannon	0
Melta cannon	10
Meltagun (model with a Ballistic Skill of 4+/other model)	5/10
Missile launcher (INFANTRY/other model)	15/20
Mortar	10
Multi-laser	5
Multi-melta (INFANTRY/other model)	20/25
Multiple rocket pod	5
Plasma cannon (INFANTRY/other model)	15/20
Plasma gun (model with a Ballistic Skill of 4+/other model)	5/10
Plasma pistol	5
Punisher gatling cannon	35
Quake cannon	0
Ripper gun	0

RANGED WEAPONS	POINTS/WEAPON
Shotgun	0
Sniper rifle	2
Storm bolter	3
Storm eagle rockets	0
Stormsword siege cannon	0
Taurox battle cannon	15
Taurox gatling cannon	20
Taurox missile launcher	30
Tremor cannon	0
Twin heavy bolter	30
Twin heavy flamer	30
Vanquisher battle cannon	15
Volcano cannon	0
Vulcan mega-bolter	0
Wyvern quad stormshard mortar	0

MELEE WEAPONS	POINTS/WEAPON
Adamantium tracks	0
Bullgryn maul	5
Chainsword	0
Force stave	0
Huge knife	0
Omnissian axe	0
Power fist	10
Power sword	5
Sentinel chainsaw	2
Telepathica stave	0
Servo-arm	0
Wyrdvane stave	0

OTHER WARGEAR	POINTS/ITEM
Augur array	5
Brute shield	0
Bullgryn plate	5
Dozer blade	5
Medi-pack	5
Platoon standard	5
Regimental standard	5
Slabshield	0
Storm shield	0
Tempestus command rod	5
Track guards	5
Vox-caster	5

ADEPTUS MECHANICUS

HQ	MODELS/UNIT	POINTS/MODEL*
Tech-Priest Dominus	1	75
Tech-Priest Enginseer	1	35
Tech-Priest Manipulus	1	70

NAMED CHARACTERS	MODELS/UNIT	POINTS/MODEL**
Belisarius Cawl	1	200

TROOPS	MODELS/UNIT	POINTS/MODEL*
Kataphron Breachers	3-12	25
Kataphron Destroyers	3-12	20
Skitarii Rangers	5-10	9
Skitarii Vanguard	5-10	9

ELITES	MODELS/UNIT	POINTS/MODEL*
Corpuscarii Electro-Priests	5-20	14
Cybernetica Datasmith	1	25
Fulgurite Electro-Priests	5-20	17
Servitors	4	7
Sicarian Infiltrators	5-10	15
Sicarian Ruststalkers	5-10	14

FAST ATTACK	MODELS/UNIT	POINTS/MODEL*
Ironstrider Ballistarii	1-6	35
Pteraxii Skystalkers	5-10	17
Pteraxii Sterylizors	5-10	19
Serberys Raiders	3-9	16
Serberys Sulphurhounds	3-9	20
Sydonian Dragoons	1-6	60

HEAVY SUPPORT	MODELS/UNIT	POINTS/MODEL*
Kastelan Robots	2-6	80
Onager Dunecrawler	1	115
Skorpius Disintegrator	1	115

DEDICATED TRANSPORT	MODELS/UNIT	POINTS/MODEL*
Skorpius Dunerider	1	80

FLYERS	MODELS/UNIT	POINTS/MODEL*
Archaeopter Fusilave	1	110
Archaeopter Stratoraptor	1	70
Archaeopter Transvector	1	100

LORDS OF WAR	MODELS/UNIT	POINTS/MODEL*
Knight Crusader	1	395
Knight Errant	1	310
Knight Gallant	1	330
Knight Paladin	1	310
Knight Warden	1	395

RANGED WEAPONS	POINTS/WEAPON
Arc pistol	5
Arc rifle	5
Archeo-revolver	0
Avenger gatling cannon	0
Belleros energy cannon	20
Cognis flamer	5
Cognis heavy stubber	5
Disruptor missile launcher	0
Eradication beamer	0
Eradication ray	10
Ferrumite cannon	25
Flechette blaster	0
Flechette carbine	0
Galvanic carbine	0
Galvanic rifle	0
Gamma pistol	10
Heavy arc rifle	5
Heavy bolter	10
Heavy flamer	0
Heavy grav-cannon	20
Heavy phosphor blaster	15
Heavy stubber	5
Icarus array	0
Incendine combustor	15
Ironstorm missile pod	15
Laspistol	0
Macrostubber	0
Magnarail lance	0
Meltagun	10
Multi-melta	20
Neutron laser	10
Phosphor blast pistol	3
Phosphor blast carbine	15
Phosphor blaster	3
Phosphor pistol	0
Phosphor serpenta	2
Phosphor torch	0
Plasma caliver	10
Plasma cannon	15
Plasma culverin	30
Radium carbine	0
Radium jezzail	0
Radium pistol	0
Rapid-fire battle cannon	100
Stormspear rocket pod	45
Stubcarbine	0
Sulphur breath	0
Thermal cannon	75
Torsion cannon	10
Transonic cannon	0
Transuranic arquebus	10
Twin cognis autocannon	30
Twin cognis heavy stubber	10
Twin cognis lascannon	40
Twin heavy phosphor blaster	0
Twin Icarus autocannon	30
Volkite blaster	5

*Excluding wargear
**Including wargear

MELEE WEAPONS	POINTS/WEAPON
Arc claw	5
Arc maul	5
Cavalry sabre	0
Chordclaw	0
Clawed limbs	0
Electroleech stave	0
Electrostatic gauntlets	0
Hydraulic claw	5
Kastelan fists	20
Mechadendrites	0
Omnissian axe	0
Omnissian staff	0
Power fist	10
Power sword	5
Pteraxii talons	0
Reaper chainsword	30
Servo-arm	0
Taser goad	5
Taser lance	10
Thunderstrike gauntlet	35
Titanic feet	0
Transonic blades	0
Transonic razor	0

OTHER WARGEAR	POINTS/ITEM
Broad spectrum data-tether	0
Chaff launcher	20
Command uplink	0
Enhanced data-tether	5
Omnispex	5
Smoke launchers	0

IMPERIAL KNIGHTS

LORDS OF WAR	MODELS/UNIT	POINTS/MODEL*
Armiger Helverin	1-3	170
Armiger Warglaive	1-3	150
Knight Castellan	1	545
Knight Crusader	1	395
Knight Errant	1	310
Knight Gallant	1	330
Knight Paladin	1	310
Knight Preceptor	1	370
Knight Valiant	1	535
Knight Warden	1	395

FORTIFICATION	MODELS/UNIT	POINTS/MODEL*
Sacristan Forgeshrine	1	85

NAMED CHARACTERS	MODELS/UNIT	POINTS/MODEL**
Canis Rex	1	430

RANGED WEAPONS	POINTS/WEAPON
Armiger autocannon	0
Avenger gatling cannon	0
Conflagration cannon	0
Heavy flamer	0
Heavy stubber	5
Ironstorm missile pod	15
Las-impulsor	0
Meltagun	10
Multi-laser	5
Plasma decimator	0
Rapid-fire battle cannon	100
Shieldbreaker missile	10
Stormspear rocket pod	45
Thermal cannon	75
Thermal spear	0
Thundercoil harpoon	0
Twin Icarus autocannon	30
Twin meltagun	0
Twin siegebreaker cannon	35
Volcano lance	0

MELEE WEAPONS	POINTS/WEAPON
Reaper chain-cleaver	0
Reaper chainsword	30
Thunderstrike gauntlet	35
Titanic feet	0

INQUISITION

HQ

HQ	MODELS/UNIT	POINTS/MODEL*
Inquisitor	1	60
Ordo Malleus Inquisitor in Terminator Armour	1	95

NAMED CHARACTERS

NAMED CHARACTERS	MODELS/UNIT	POINTS/MODEL**
Inquisitor Coteaz	1	95
Inquisitor Eisenhorn	1	85
Inquisitor Greyfax	1	90
Inquisitor Karamazov	1	125
Lord Inquisitor Kyria Draxus	1	85

ELITES

ELITES	MODELS/UNIT	POINTS/MODEL*
Acolytes	1-6	9
Daemonhost	1	25
Jokaero Weaponsmith	1	20

RANGED WEAPONS

RANGED WEAPONS	POINTS/WEAPON
Bolt pistol	0
Boltgun	0
Combi-flamer	10
Combi-melta	10
Combi-plasma	10
Condemnor boltgun	5

RANGED WEAPONS	POINTS/WEAPON
Digital weapons	5
Flamer	5
Frag grenade	0
Hot-shot lasgun	0
Incinerator	15
Inferno pistol	5
Laspistol	0
Krak grenade	0
Meltagun	14
Needle pistol	2
Plasma gun	11
Plasma pistol	5
Psycannon	10
Psyk-out grenade	0
Storm bolter	3
Unholy gaze	0

MELEE WEAPONS

MELEE WEAPONS	POINTS/WEAPON
Chainsword	0
Force axe	10
Force stave	10
Force sword	10
Nemesis Daemon hammer	20
Power fist	10
Power maul	5
Power sword	5
Thunder hammer	15
Warp grasp	0

FORCES OF CHAOS

CHAOS SPACE MARINES

HQ	MODELS/UNIT	POINTS/MODEL*
Chaos Lord	1	80
Chaos Lord in Terminator Armour	1	95
Chaos Lord with Jump Pack	1	105
Daemon Prince	1	150
Daemon Prince with Wings	1	185
Dark Apostle	1	80
Exalted Champion	1	75
Lord Discordant on Helstalker	1	180
Master of Executions	1	65
Master of Possession	1	95
Sorcerer	1	90
Sorcerer in Terminator Armour	1	105
Sorcerer with Jump Pack	1	115
Warpsmith	1	50

NAMED CHARACTERS	MODELS/UNIT	POINTS/MODEL**
Abaddon the Despoiler	1	220
Cypher	1	85
Fabius Bile	1	90
- Surgeon Acolyte	0-1	5
Haarken Worldclaimer	1	95
Huron Blackheart	1	110
Khârn the Betrayer	1	115
Lucius the Eternal	1	90

TROOPS	MODELS/UNIT	POINTS/MODEL*
Chaos Cultists	10-30	6
Chaos Space Marines	5-20	14

ELITES	MODELS/UNIT	POINTS/MODEL*
Chosen	5-10	15
Dark Disciples	2	5
Fallen	5-10	14
Greater Possessed	1-2	65
Helbrute	1	70
Khorne Berzerkers	5-20	17

* Excluding wargear
** Including wargear
*** Including weapons, but not other wargear

ELITES	MODELS/UNIT	POINTS/MODEL*
Mutilators	3	35
Noise Marines	5-20	16
Plague Marines	5-20	18
Possessed	5-20	20
Rubric Marines	5-20	18
Terminators	5-10	23

FAST ATTACK	MODELS/UNIT	POINTS/MODEL*
Bikers	3-9	25
Chaos Spawn	1-5	23
Raptors	5-15	18
Warp Talons	5-10	17

HEAVY SUPPORT	MODELS/UNIT	POINTS/MODEL*
Chaos Land Raider	1	175
Chaos Predator	1	90
Chaos Vindicator	1	130
Defiler	1	120
Forgefiend	1	85
Havocs	5	17
Maulerfiend	1	130
Obliterators	1-3	105
Venomcrawler	1	130

DEDICATED TRANSPORT	MODELS/UNIT	POINTS/MODEL*
Chaos Rhino	1	75

LORDS OF WAR	MODELS/UNIT	POINTS/MODEL*
Khorne Lord of Skulls	1	350

FLYERS	MODELS/UNIT	POINTS/MODEL*
Heldrake	1	130

FORTIFICATIONS	MODELS/UNIT	POINTS/MODEL*
Noctilith Crown	1	85

DAEMONS	MODELS/UNIT	POINTS/MODEL***
Bloodletters	10-30	8
Daemonettes	10-30	7
Horrors	10-30	
- Blue Horrors		7
- Pairs of Brimstone Horrors		5
- Pink Horrors		8
- Iridescent Horror		8
Plaguebearers	10-30	9

RANGED WEAPONS	POINTS/WEAPON
Autocannon (INFANTRY/other model)	10/15
Autogun	0
Autopistol	0
Baleflamer	20
Battle cannon	0
Blastmaster	10
Blight launcher	10
Bolt pistol	0
Boltgun	0

RANGED WEAPONS	POINTS/WEAPON
Combi-bolter	3
Combi-flamer	10
Combi-melta	10
Combi-plasma	10
Daemongore cannon	40
Demolisher cannon	0
Doom siren	10
Ectoplasma cannon	20
Excruciator cannon	0
Flamer	5
Fleshmetal guns	0
Gorestorm cannon	30
Hades autocannon	25
Hades gatling cannon	90
Havoc launcher	5
Heavy bolter (INFANTRY/other model)	10/15
Heavy flamer (INFANTRY/other model)	10/15
Heavy stubber	5
Helbrute plasma cannon	20
Ichor cannon	25
Inferno bolt pistol	0
Inferno boltgun	0
Lascannon (INFANTRY/other model)	15/20
Lashing warp energies	0
Magma cutter	5
Meltagun	10
Missile launcher (INFANTRY/other model)	15/20
Multi-melta (INFANTRY/other model)	20/25
Plague belcher	5
Plague spewer	10
Plasma gun	10
Plasma pistol	5
Predator autocannon	40
Reaper autocannon	10
Reaper chaincannon	20
Shotgun	0
Skullhurler	60
Sonic blaster	5
Soulreaper cannon	10
Twin heavy bolter	30
Twin heavy flamer	30
Twin lascannon	40
Warp bolter	5
Warpflame pistol	5
Warpflamer	8

MELEE WEAPONS	POINTS/WEAPON
Accursed crozius	0
Axe of dismemberment	0
Bladed limbs and tail	0
Brutal assault weapon	0
Bubotic axe	5
Chainaxe	1
Chainfist	10
Chainsword	0
Crushing fists	0
Daemon jaws	0
Daemonic axe	10
Daemonic mutations	0
Defiler claws	0
Defiler scourge	10
Eviscerating claws	0
Flail of corruption	15

MELEE WEAPONS	POINTS/WEAPON	MELEE WEAPONS	POINTS/WEAPON
Fleshmetal weapons	0	Power axe	5
Force axe	0	Power fist	10
Force stave	0	Power maul	5
Force sword	0	Power scourge	25
Great cleaver of Khorne	0	Power sword	5
Great plague cleaver	15	Soulflayer tendrils	0
Helbrute fist (single/pair)	20/30	Techno-virus injector	0
Helbrute hammer	30	Thunder hammer (CHARACTER/other model)	40/15
Heldrake claws	0		
Hellforged sword	10		
Hideous mutations	0	OTHER WARGEAR	POINTS/ITEM
Horrifying mutations	0	Blight grenades	0
Impaler chainglaive	0	Daemonic Icon	15
Lasher tendrils	10	Frag grenades	0
Lightning claws (single/pair)	5/10	Icon of Despair	10
Mace of contagion	5	Icon of Excess	10
Malefic talons (one set/two sets)	0/15	Icon of Flame	5
Maulerfiend fists	0	Icon of Vengeance	5
Mechatendrils	0	Icon of Wrath	10
Plague knife	0	Instrument of Chaos	10
Plaguesword	0	Krak grenades	0

DEATH GUARD

HQ	MODELS/UNIT	POINTS/MODEL*
Chaos Lord	1	80
Chaos Lord in Terminator Armour	1	95
Daemon Prince of Nurgle	1	150
Daemon Prince of Nurgle with Wings	1	185
Lord of Contagion	1	100
Malignant Plaguecaster	1	100
Sorcerer	1	90
Sorcerer in Terminator Armour	1	105

NAMED CHARACTERS	MODELS/UNIT	POINTS/MODEL***
Mortarion	1	490
Typhus	1	165

TROOPS	MODELS/UNIT	POINTS/MODEL*
Chaos Cultists	10-40	6
Plague Marines	5-20	18
Poxwalkers	10-20	7

ELITES	MODELS/UNIT	POINTS/MODEL*
Biologus Putrifier	1	65
Blightlord Terminators	5-10	35
Deathshroud Terminators	3-6	32
Foul Blightspawn	1	85
Helbrute	1	70
Noxious Blightbringer	1	55
Plague Surgeon	1	60
Possessed	5-20	20
Tallyman	1	55

FAST ATTACK	MODELS/UNIT	POINTS/MODEL*
Chaos Spawn	1-5	23
Foetid Bloat-drone	1	115
Myphitic Blight-haulers	1-3	55

HEAVY SUPPORT	MODELS/UNIT	POINTS/MODEL*
Chaos Land Raider	1	175
Chaos Predator	1	90
Defiler	1	120
Plagueburst Crawler	1	130

DEDICATED TRANSPORT	MODELS/UNIT	POINTS/MODEL*
Chaos Rhino	1	75

DAEMONS	MODELS/UNIT	POINTS/MODEL***
Beasts of Nurgle	1-9	34
Nurglings	3-9	20
Plaguebearers	10-30	9
Plague Drones	3-9	40

*Excluding wargear
** Including wargear
*** Including weapons, but not other wargear

RANGED WEAPONS	POINTS/WEAPON	MELEE WEAPONS	POINTS/WEAPON
Autogun	0	Balesword	5
Autopistol	0	Brutal assault weapon	0
Battle cannon	0	Bubotic axe	5
Bile spurt	0	Chainaxe	1
Blight grenades	0	Chainfist	10
Blight launcher	10	Chainsword	0
Bolt pistol	0	Corrupted staff	0
Boltgun	0	Cursed plague bell	0
Combi-bolter	3	Daemonic axe	10
Combi-flamer	10	Defiler claws	0
Combi-melta	10	Defiler scourge	10
Combi-plasma	10	Flail of corruption	15
Entropy cannon	15	Fleshmower	10
Flamer	5	Force axe	0
Havoc launcher	5	Force stave	0
Heavy blight launcher	25	Force sword	0
Heavy bolter	10	Gnashing maw	0
Heavy flamer	10	Great plague cleaver	15
Heavy slugger	0	Helbrute fist (single/pair)	20/30
Heavy stubber	5	Helbrute hammer	30
Helbrute plasma cannon	20	Hellforged sword	10
Hyper blight grenades	0	Hideous mutations	0
Injector pistol	0	Horrifying mutations	0
Krak grenades	0	Improvised weapon	0
Lascannon	20	Lightning claws (single/pair)	5/10
Meltagun	10	Mace of contagion	5
Missile launcher	20	Malefic talons (one set/two sets)	0/15
Multi-melta	25	Manreaper	15
Plague belcher	5	Plague knife	0
Plagueburst mortar	0	Plague probe	0
Plague spewer	10	Plaguesword	0
Plaguespitter	20	Plaguereaper	20
Plague sprayer	0	Power axe	5
Plaguespurt gauntlet	0	Power fist	10
Plasma gun	10	Power maul	5
Plasma pistol	5	Power scourge	25
Predator autocannon	40	Power sword	5
Reaper autocannon	10		
Rothail volley gun	5		
Shotgun	0	**OTHER WARGEAR**	**POINTS/ITEM**
Twin heavy bolter	30		
Twin heavy flamer	30	Daemonic Icon	15
Twin lascannon	40	Icon of Despair	10
		Instrument of Chaos	10

THOUSAND SONS

HQ	MODELS/UNIT	POINTS/MODEL*
Daemon Prince of Tzeentch	1	150
Daemon Prince of Tzeentch with Wings	1	185
Exalted Sorcerer	1	100
Exalted Sorcerer on Disc of Tzeentch	1	120
Sorcerer	1	90
Sorcerer in Terminator Armour	1	105

NAMED CHARACTERS	MODELS/UNIT	POINTS/MODEL**
Ahriman	1	150
Ahriman on Disc of Tzeentch	1	170
Magnus the Red	1	465

TROOPS	MODELS/UNIT	POINTS/MODEL*
Chaos Cultists	10-40	6
Rubric Marines	5-20	18
Tzaangors	10-30	9

ELITES	MODELS/UNIT	POINTS/MODEL*
Helbrute	1	70
Scarab Occult Terminators	5-10	30
Tzaangor Shaman	1	85

25

FAST ATTACK	MODELS/UNIT	POINTS/MODEL*
Chaos Spawn	1-5	23
Tzaangor Enlightened	3-9	18

HEAVY SUPPORT	MODELS/UNIT	POINTS/MODEL*
Chaos Land Raider	1	175
Chaos Predator	1	90
Chaos Vindicator	1	130
Defiler	1	120
Forgefiend	1	85
Maulerfiend	1	130
Mutalith Vortex Beast	1	135

DEDICATED TRANSPORT	MODELS/UNIT	POINTS/MODEL*
Chaos Rhino	1	75

FLYERS	MODELS/UNIT	POINTS/MODEL*
Heldrake	1	130

DAEMONS	MODELS/UNIT	POINTS/MODEL***
Flamers	3-9	23
Horrors	10-30	
- Blue Horrors		7
- Pairs of Brimstone Horrors		5
- Pink Horrors		8
- Iridescent Horror		8
Screamers	3-9	26

RANGED WEAPONS	POINTS/WEAPON
Autogun	0
Autopistol	0
Baleflamer	20
Battle cannon	0
Combi-bolter	3
Combi-flamer	10
Combi-melta	10
Demolisher cannon	0
Ectoplasma cannon	20
Fatecaster greatbow	2
Flamer	5
Frag grenades	0
Hades autocannon	25
Havoc launcher	5
Heavy bolter	15
Heavy flamer	15
Heavy stubber	5
Heavy warpflamer	15
Helbrute plasma cannon	20
Hellfyre missile rack	15
Inferno bolt pistol	0
Inferno boltgun	0
Inferno combi-bolter	3
Krak grenades	0
Lascannon	20
Magma cutter	5
Missile launcher	20
Multi-melta	25
Plasma pistol	5
Predator autocannon	40

RANGED WEAPONS	POINTS/WEAPON
Reaper autocannon	10
Shotgun	0
Soulreaper cannon	10
Twin heavy bolter	30
Twin heavy flamer	30
Twin lascannon	40
Warpflame pistol	5
Warpflamer	8

MELEE WEAPONS	POINTS/WEAPON
Betentacled maw	0
Brutal assault weapon	0
Chainsword	0
Daemon jaws	0
Daemonic axe	10
Defiler claws	0
Defiler scourge	10
Divining spear	0
Enormous claws	0
Force stave	0
Force sword	0
Helbrute fist (single/pair)	20/30
Helbrute hammer	30
Heldrake claws	0
Hellforged sword	10
Hideous mutations	0
Lasher tendrils	10
Malefic talons (one set/two sets)	0/15
Maulerfiend fists	0
Power scourge	25
Power sword	5
Tzaangor blades	0

OTHER WARGEAR	POINTS/ITEM
Brayhorn	10
Daemonic Icon	15
Familiar	10
Icon of Flame	5
Instrument of Chaos	10

* Excluding wargear
** Including wargear
*** Including weapons, but not other wargear

CHAOS DAEMONS

HQ	MODELS/UNIT	POINTS/MODEL***
Be'lakor	1	220
Bloodmaster	1	60
Bloodthirster of Insensate Rage	1	250
Bloodthirster of Unfettered Fury	1	240
Blood Throne	1	115
The Blue Scribes	1	90
Changecaster	1	85
The Changeling	1	105
Contorted Epitome	1	210
Epidemius	1	105
Fateskimmer	1	160
Fluxmaster	1	105
Great Unclean one with:		
- Bilesword and bileblade	1	260
- Bilesword and plague flail	1	270
- Doomsday bell and bileblade	1	270
- Doomsday bell and plague flail	1	280
Herald of Slaanesh	1	55
Herald of Slaanesh on Exalted Seeker Chariot	1	130
Herald of Slaanesh on Hellflayer	1	105
Herald of Slaanesh on Seeker Chariot	1	95
Horticulous Slimux	1	160
Infernal Enrapturess	1	75
Kairos Fateweaver	1	270
Karanak	1	75
Keeper of Secrets with:		
- Living whip	1	230
- Ritual knife	1	230
- Shining aegis	1	240
- Sinistrous hand	1	230
Lord of Change	1	270
Lord of Change with baleful sword	1	275
The Masque of Slaanesh	1	85
Poxbringer	1	75
Rotigus	1	270
Shalaxi Helbane with:		
- Living whip	1	240
- Shining aegis	1	250
Skarbrand	1	310
Skullmaster	1	95
Skulltaker	1	90
Sloppity Bilepiper	1	65
Spoilpox Scrivener	1	100
Syll'Esske, the Vengeful Allegiance	1	230
Wrath of Khorne Bloodthirster	1	230

DAEMON PRINCES		POINTS/MODEL*
Daemon Prince of Chaos	1	150
Daemon Prince with Wings	1	185

TROOPS	MODELS/UNIT	POINTS/MODEL***
Bloodletters	10-30	8
Daemonettes	10-30	7
Horrors	10-30	
- Blue Horrors		7
- Pairs of Brimstone Horrors		5
- Pink Horrors		8
- Iridescent Horror		8
Nurglings	3-9	18
Plaguebearers	10-30	9

FAST ATTACK	MODELS/UNIT	POINTS/MODEL***
Chaos Spawn	1	23
Furies	5-20	9
Flesh Hounds	5-20	18 (Gore Hounds are 28)
Hellflayer	1	80
Plague Drones	3-9	40
Screamers	3-9	26
Seekers	5-20	18

ELITES	MODELS/UNIT	POINTS/MODEL***
Beasts of Nurgle	1-9	35
Bloodcrushers	3-12	45
Exalted Flamer	1	60
Fiends	1-9	40 (Blissbringer is 45)
Flamers	3-9	23

HEAVY SUPPORT	MODELS/UNIT	POINTS/MODEL***
Burning Chariot	1	110
Exalted Seeker Chariot	1	80
Seeker Chariot	1	60
Skull Altar	1	110
Skull Cannon	1	90
Soul Grinder	1	190

FORTIFICATIONS	MODELS/UNIT	POINTS/MODEL***
Feculent Gnarlmaws	1-3	95

MELEE WEAPONS	POINTS/WEAPON
Daemonic axe	10
Hellforged sword	10
Malefic talons (one set/two sets)	0/15

OTHER WARGEAR	POINTS/ITEM
Chanting Horrors (for Burning Chariot and Fateskimmer)	5
Daemonic Icon	15
Instrument of Chaos	10
Rod of sorcery (for Lord of Change)	10
Staff of change	5

* Excluding wargear
** Including wargear
*** Including weapons, but not other wargear

CHAOS KNIGHTS

LORDS OF WAR	MODELS/UNIT	POINTS/MODEL*
Knight Desecrator	1	370
Knight Despoiler	1	310
Knight Despoiler with 1 reaper chainsword and 1 thunderstrike gauntlet	1	330
Knight Rampager	1	345
Knight Tyrant	1	535
War Dog	1-3	150

RANGED WEAPONS		POINTS/WEAPON
Avenger gatling cannon (single/pair)		90/200
Conflagration cannon		0
Heavy flamer		0
Heavy stubber		5
Ironstorm missile pod		15
Laser destructor		0
Meltagun		10
Multi-laser		5
Plasma decimator		40

RANGED WEAPONS	POINTS/WEAPON
Rapid-fire battle cannon	100
Shieldbreaker missile	10
Stormspear rocket pod	45
Thermal cannon	75
Thermal spear	0
Thundercoil harpoon	0
Twin Icarus autocannon	30
Twin meltagun	0
Twin siegebreaker cannon	35
Volcano lance	70
War Dog autocannon	10

MELEE WEAPONS	POINTS/WEAPON
Reaper chain-cleaver	0
Reaper chainsword	30
Thunderstrike gauntlet	35
Titanic feet	0

FORCES OF THE XENOS

CRAFTWORLDS

HQ	MODELS/UNIT	POINTS/MODEL*
Autarch	1	80
Autarch Skyrunner	1	105
Autarch with Swooping Hawk Wings	1	90
Farseer	1	115
Farseer Skyrunner	1	135
Spiritseer	1	60
Warlock	1	50
Warlock Conclave	2-10	40
Warlock Skyrunner	1	65
Warlock Skyrunner Conclave	2-10	55

NAMED CHARACTERS	MODELS/UNIT	POINTS/MODEL**
Asurmen	1	160
Avatar of Khaine	1	235
Baharroth	1	120
Eldrad Ulthran	1	155
Fuegan	1	135
Illic Nightspear	1	70
Jain Zar	1	125
Karandras	1	135
Maugan Ra	1	150
Prince Yriel	1	85

DEDICATED TRANSPORT	MODELS/UNIT	POINTS/MODEL*
Wave Serpent	1	130

TROOPS	MODELS/UNIT	POINTS/MODEL*
Dire Avengers	5-10	13
Guardian Defenders	10-20	10
- Heavy Weapon Platform	0-2	12
Rangers	5-10	15
Storm Guardians	8-24	9

ELITES	MODELS/UNIT	POINTS/MODEL*
Fire Dragons	5-10	23
Howling Banshees	5-10	15
Striking Scorpions	5-10	13
Wraithblades	5-10	40
Wraithguard	5-10	38

FAST ATTACK	MODELS/UNIT	POINTS/MODEL*
Shining Spears	3-9	35
Swooping Hawks	5-10	16
Vypers	1-3	40
Warp Spiders	5-10	18
Windriders	3-9	20

FLYERS	MODELS/UNIT	POINTS/MODEL*
Crimson Hunter	1	140
Crimson Hunter Exarch	1	170
Hemlock Wraithfighter	1	230

* Excluding wargear
** Including wargear

HEAVY SUPPORT	MODELS/UNIT	POINTS/MODEL*
Dark Reapers	3-10	35
Falcon	1	115
Fire Prism	1	170
Night Spinner	1	145
Support Weapons (including crew)	1-3	30
War Walkers	1-3	40
Wraithlord	1	100

LORDS OF WAR	MODELS/UNIT	POINTS/MODEL*
Wraithknight	1	315

FORTIFICATIONS	MODELS/UNIT	POINTS/MODEL*
Webway Gate	1	95

RANGED WEAPONS	POINTS/WEAPON
Aeldari missile launcher	20
Avenger shuriken catapult (single/pair)	0/5
Bright lance	20
D-cannon	40
D-scythe	10
Death spinner (single/pair)	0/5
Doomweaver	0
Dragon's breath flamer	10
Firepike	15
Flamer	5
Fusion gun (FIRE DRAGON/other model)	0/10
Fusion pistol	0
Hawk's talon	5
Heavy D-scythe	0
Heavy wraithcannon	50
Lasblaster	0
Laser lance (AUTARCH SKYRUNNER/other model)	5/0
Melta bomb	0
Plasma grenade	0
Prism cannon	0
Pulse laser	0
Ranger long rifle	0
Reaper launcher	0
Scatter laser	10
Scorpion's claw	10
Shadow weaver	20
Shuriken cannon (Dark Reaper Exarch/other model)	0/10
Shuriken catapult	0
Shuriken pistol	0
Singing spear	5
Star lance	5
Starcannon	15
Suncannon	60
Tempest launcher	10
Triskele	5
Twin Aeldari missile launcher	40
Twin bright lance	40
Twin scatter laser	20
Twin shuriken cannon	20
Twin shuriken catapult	0
Twin starcannon	30
Vibro cannon	15
Wraithcannon	0

MELEE WEAPONS	POINTS/WEAPON
Aeldari blade	0
Biting blade	5
Chainsword	0
Diresword	0
Executioner	5
Ghostaxe	0
Ghostglaive	10
Ghostswords	0
Mirrorswords	0
Paragon sabre	0
Power glaive	0
Power sword (Swooping Hawk Exarch/other model)	5/0
Powerblades	5
Scorpion chainsword	0
Star glaive	0
Titanic feet	0
Titanic ghostglaive	30
Titanic wraithbone fists	0
Witchblade	0
Witch staff	0
Wraithbone fists	0
Wraithguard fists	0

OTHER WARGEAR	POINTS/ITEM
Crystal targeting matrix	5
Forceshield	0
Scattershield	15
Shimmershield	5
Spirit stones	10
Star engines	10
Vectored engines	10

DRUKHARI

HQ	MODELS/UNIT	POINTS/MODEL*
Archon	1	60
Haemonculus	1	75
Succubus	1	55

NAMED CHARACTERS	MODELS/UNIT	POINTS/MODEL**
Drazhar	1	105
Lelith Hesperax	1	85
Urien Rakarth	1	95

TROOPS	MODELS/UNIT	POINTS/MODEL*
Kabalite Warriors	5-20	9
Wracks	5-10	12
Wyches	5-20	11

FAST ATTACK	MODELS/UNIT	POINTS/MODEL*
Clawed Fiends	1-6	35
Hellions	5-20	15
Khymerae	2-12	12
Razorwing Flocks	1-12	14
Reavers	3-12	20
Scourges	5-10	15

ELITES	MODELS/UNIT	POINTS/MODEL*
Beastmaster	1	40
Grotesques	3-10	40
Incubi	5-10	16
Lhamaean	1	16
Mandrakes	5-10	17
Medusae	1	22
Sslyth	1	21
Ur-Ghul	1	16

HEAVY SUPPORT	MODELS/UNIT	POINTS/MODEL*
Cronos	1-3	70
Ravager	1	85
Talos	1-3	85

DEDICATED TRANSPORTS	MODELS/UNIT	POINTS/MODEL*
Raider	1	70
Venom	1	60

FLYERS	MODELS/UNIT	POINTS/MODEL*
Razorwing Jetfighter	1	120
Voidraven Bomber	1	185

FORTIFICATIONS	MODELS/UNIT	POINTS/MODEL*
Webway Gate	1	95

RANGED WEAPONS	POINTS/WEAPON
Baleblast	0
Blast pistol	5
Blaster	15
Dark lance (INFANTRY/other model)	15/20
Dark scythe	0
Disintegrator cannon	25
Eyeburst	0
Haywire blaster	10
Heat lance	10
Hexrifle	5
Liquifier gun	10
Ossefactor	5
Phantasm grenade launcher	5
Razorwing missiles	0
Shardcarbine	0
Shredder	10
Spirit syphon	0
Spirit vortex	10
Splinter cannon (INFANTRY/other model)	10/15
Splinter pistol	0
Splinter pods	0
Splinter rifle	0
Stinger pistol	5
Stinger pod	10
Twin liquifier gun	15
Twin splinter rifle	0
Void lance	0
Voidraven missiles	0

MELEE WEAPONS	POINTS/WEAPON
Agoniser	5
Archite glaive	0
Bladevanes	0
Chain-flails	5
Clawed fists	0
Claws and talons	0
Electrocorrosive whip	5
Demiklaives	0
Flesh gauntlet	5
Glimmersteel blade	0
Haemonculus tools	0
Hekatarii blade	0
Hellglaive	0
Huskblade	5
Hydra gauntlets	5
Ichor injector	5
Impaler	5
Klaive	0
Macro-scalpel	5
Mindphase gauntlet	5
Monstrous cleaver	0
Power lance	5
Power sword	5
Razor feathers	0
Razorflails	5
Scissorhand	10
Shaimeshi blade	0
Shardnet and impaler	10
Shock prow	5
Spirit-leech tentacles	0
Sslyth battle-blade	0
Stunclaw	5
Talos gauntlet	15
Venom blade	5

OTHER WARGEAR	POINTS/ITEM
Chain-snares	2
Cluster caltrops	3
Grav-talon	3
Grisly trophies	2
Spirit probe	5
Splinter racks	10

Excluding wargear
** Including wargear

HARLEQUINS

HQ	MODELS/UNIT	POINTS/MODEL*
Shadowseer	1	115
Troupe Master	1	65

TROOPS	MODELS/UNIT	POINTS/MODEL*
Troupe	5-12	14

ELITES	MODELS/UNIT	POINTS/MODEL*
Death Jester	1	50
Solitaire	1	90

FAST ATTACK	MODELS/UNIT	POINTS/MODEL*
Skyweavers	2-6	35

HEAVY SUPPORT	MODELS/UNIT	POINTS/MODEL*
Voidweaver	1	65

DEDICATED TRANSPORT	MODELS/UNIT	POINTS/MODEL*
Starweaver	1	60

FORTIFICATIONS	MODELS/UNIT	POINTS/MODEL*
Webway Gate	1	95

RANGED WEAPONS	POINTS/WEAPON
Fusion pistol	5
Hallucinogen grenade launcher	0
Haywire cannon	15
Neuro disruptor	5
Prismatic cannon	15
Plasma grenades	0
Shrieker cannon	0
Shuriken cannon	10
Shuriken pistol	0
Star bolas	0

MELEE WEAPONS	POINTS/WEAPON
Harlequin's blade	0
Harlequin's caress	6
Harlequin's embrace	5
Harlequin's kiss	6
Miststave	0
Power sword	5
Zephyrglaive	5

YNNARI

NAMED CHARACTER	MODELS/UNIT	POINTS/MODEL**
The Visarch	1	85
The Yncarne	1	290
Yvraine	1	120

NECRONS

HQ	MODELS/UNIT	POINTS/MODEL*
Catacomb Command Barge	1	145
Cryptek	1	85
Destroyer Lord	1	110
Lord	1	70
Overlord	1	85

NAMED CHARACTERS	MODELS/UNIT	POINTS/MODEL**
Anrakyr the Traveller	1	130
C'tan Shard of the Deceiver	1	190
C'tan Shard of the Nightbringer	1	165
Illuminor Szeras	1	145
Imotekh the Stormlord	1	150
Nemesor Zahndrekh	1	135
Orikan the Diviner	1	110
Trazyn the Infinite	1	100
Vargard Obyron	1	120

TROOPS	MODELS/UNIT	POINTS/MODEL*
Immortals	5-10	18
Necron Warriors	10-20	12

ELITES	MODELS/UNIT	POINTS/MODEL*
Deathmarks	5-10	16
Flayed Ones	5-20	14
Lychguard	5-10	30
Triarch Praetorians	5-10	23
Triarch Stalker	1	95

FAST ATTACK	MODELS/UNIT	POINTS/MODEL*
Canoptek Scarabs	3-9	15
Canoptek Wraiths	3-6	45
Destroyers	1-6	55 (Heavy Destroyer is 40)
Tomb Blades	3-9	17

HEAVY SUPPORT	MODELS/UNIT	POINTS/MODEL*
Annihilation Barge	1	115
Doomsday Ark	1	180
Heavy Destroyers	1-3	40
Monolith	1	270
Transcendent C'tan	1	195

DEDICATED TRANSPORTS	MODELS/UNIT	POINTS/MODEL*
Ghost Ark	1	140

FLYERS	MODELS/UNIT	POINTS/MODEL*
Doom Scythe	1	170
Night Scythe	1	135

LORDS OF WAR	MODELS/UNIT	POINTS/MODEL*
Obelisk	1	390
Tesseract Vault	1	550

RANGED WEAPONS	POINTS/WEAPON
Death ray	0
Doomsday cannon	0
Gauss blaster (single/pair)	0/15
Gauss cannon (VEHICLE/other model)	5/0
Gauss flayer	0
Gauss flayer array	0
Gauss flux arc	0
Heat ray	30
Heavy gauss cannon	0
Particle beamer	10
Particle caster	0
Particle shredder	25
Particle whip	0
Rod of covenant	0
Staff of light	0
Synaptic disintegrator	0
Tesla cannon	0
Tesla carbine (single/pair)	0/15
Tesla destructor	0
Tesla sphere	0
Transdimensional beamer	15
Twin heavy gauss cannon	40
Twin tesla destructor	0

MELEE WEAPONS	POINTS/WEAPON
Automaton claws	0
Crackling tendrils	0
Feeder mandibles	0
Flayer claws	0
Hyperphase sword	0
Massive forelimbs	0
Vicious claws	0
Voidblade	0
Voidscythe	5
Warscythe	0
Whip coils	5

OTHER WARGEAR	POINTS/ITEM
Canoptek cloak	10
Chronometron	15
Dispersion shield	0
Fabricator claw array	5
Gloom prism	5
Nebuloscope	3
Phylactery	10
Resurrection orb	20
Shadowloom	5
Shieldvanes	3

ORKS

HQ	MODELS/UNIT	POINTS/MODEL*
Big Mek in Mega Armour	1	85
- Grot Oiler	0-1	5
Big Mek with Shokk Attack Gun	1	95
- Grot Oiler	0-1	5
Big Mek with Kustom Force Field	1	60
- Grot Oiler	0-1	5
Deffkilla Wartrike	1	125
Warboss	1	70
Weirdboy	1	75

NAMED CHARACTERS	MODELS/UNIT	POINTS/MODEL**
Boss Snikrot	1	75
Boss Zagstruk	1	95
Ghazghkull Thraka	1	300
Makari	1	65
Kaptin Badrukk	1	90
- Ammo Runt	0-1	5
Mad Dok Grotsnik	1	90

TROOPS	MODELS/UNIT	POINTS/MODEL*
Boyz	10-30	8
Gretchin	10-30	5

ELITES	MODELS/UNIT	POINTS/MODEL*
Burna Boyz	5-15	11
Kommandos	5-15	9
Meganobz	3-10	25
Mek	1	25
- Grot Oiler	0-1	5
Nob with Waaagh! Banner	1	85
Nobz	5-10	17
- Ammo Runts	0-2	5
Nobz on Warbikes	3-9	35
Painboy	1	55
Runtherd	1	40
Tankbustas	5-15	7
- Bomb Squigs	0-6	10

FAST ATTACK	MODELS/UNIT	POINTS/MODEL*
Boomdakka Snazzwagons	1-3	85
Deffkoptas	1-5	25
Kustom Boosta-blastas	1-3	90
Megatrakk Scrapjets	1-3	90
Rukkatrukk Squigbuggies	1-3	110
Shokkjump Dragstas	1-3	100
Stormboyz	5-30	12
Warbikers	3-12	27

DEDICATED TRANSPORTS	MODELS/UNIT	POINTS/MODEL*
Trukk	1	60

HEAVY SUPPORT	MODELS/UNIT	POINTS/MODEL*
Battlewagon	1	135
Bonebreaka	1	160
Deff Dreads	1-3	55
Flash Gitz	5-10	32
- Ammo Runts	0-2	5
Gorkanaut	1	285
Gunwagon	1	160
Killa Kans	1-6	45
Lootas	5-15	20
Mek Gunz (including krew)	1-6	20
Morkanaut	1	270

FLYERS	MODELS/UNIT	POINTS/MODEL*
Blitza-bommer	1	130
Burna-bommer	1	125
Dakkajet	1	110
Wazbom Blastajet	1	140

LORDS OF WAR	MODELS/UNIT	POINTS/MODEL*
Stompa	1	850

FORTIFICATIONS	MODELS/UNIT	POINTS/MODEL**
Mekboy Workshop	1	85

RANGED WEAPONS	POINTS/WEAPON
Big shoota	5
Bubblechukka	30
Burna	0
Burna bottles	0
Burna exhaust	0
Dakkagun	0
Deffgun	0
Deffkannon	0
Deffstorm mega-shoota	0
Grot blasta	0
Grotzooka	10
Heavy squig launcha	0
Kannon	15
Killa jet	0
Killkannon	15
Kombi-weapon with rokkit launcha	10
Kombi-weapon with skorcha	15
Kopta rokkits	25
Kustom mega-blasta	10
Kustom mega-kannon	45
Kustom mega-slugga	5
Kustom mega-zappa	0
Kustom shokk rifle	0
Kustom shoota	3
Lobba	20
Mek speshul	0
Rivet kannon	0
Rokkit kannon	0
Rokkit launcha	10
Pair of rokkit pistols	10
Shokk attack gun	25
Shoota	0
Shotgun	0
Skorcha	15
Skorcha missiles	10

RANGED WEAPONS	POINTS/WEAPON
Slugga	0
Smasha gun	20
Snagga klaw	0
Snazzgun	0
Squig bomb	0
Squig launcha	0
Stikkbomb chukka	5
Stikkbomb flinga	5
Stikkbombs	0
Stikksquigs	0
Supa-shoota	10
Supa-gatler	0
Supa-rokkit	5
Tankbusta bombs	0
Tellyport blasta	10
Tellyport mega-blasta	10
Traktor kannon	30
Twin big shoota	10
Twin boomstikk	0
Wazbom mega-kannon	0
Wing missiles	0
Zzap gun	15

MELEE WEAPONS	POINTS/WEAPON
Attack squig	0
Big choppa	5
Buzz saw	0
Choppa	0
Deff rolla	20
Dread klaw	15
Dread saw	10
Drilla	0
Grabba stikk	0
Grabbin' klaw	5
Grot-prod	0
Kan klaw	0
Killsaw (single/pair)	10/15
Klaw of Gork (or possibly Mork)	0
Mega-choppa	0
Nose drill	0
Power klaw	10
Power stabba	5
Saw blades	0
Spinnin' blades	0
Tankhammer	10
'Urty syringe	0
Waaagh! banner	0
Weirdboy staff	0
Wreckin' ball	5

OTHER WARGEAR	POINTS/ITEM
'Ard case	0
Cybork body	5
Gitfinda squig	0
Grot lash	0
Grot rigger	5
Kustom force field	20
Squig hound	0

* Excluding wargear
** Including wargear

T'AU EMPIRE

HQ	MODELS/UNIT	POINTS/MODEL†
Cadre Fireblade	1	45
Commander in XV8 Crisis Battlesuit	1	85
Commander in XV85 Enforcer Battlesuit	1	90
Commander in XV86 Coldstar Battlesuit	1	110
Ethereal	1	55
Ethereal with Hover Drone	1	60
Longstrike	1	185

NAMED CHARACTERS	MODELS/UNIT	POINTS/MODEL†††
Aun'Shi	1	55
Aun'Va	1	75
- Ethereal Guard	2	5
Commander Farsight	1	130
Commander Shadowsun	1	135
Darkstrider	1	60
The Eight	8 Characters, 14 Drones	1250

TROOPS	MODELS/UNIT	POINTS/MODEL†
Breacher Team	5-10	9
- DS8 Tactical Support Turret	0-1	0
Kroot Carnivores	10-20	6
Strike Team	5-12	9
- DS8 Tactical Support Turret	0-1	0

ELITES	MODELS/UNIT	POINTS/MODEL†
XV8 Crisis Battlesuits	3-9	30
XV8 Crisis Bodyguards	3-9	33
Firesight Marksman	1	30
XV95 Ghostkeel Battlesuit	1	110
Krootox Riders	1-3	28
Kroot Shaper	1	25
XV104 Riptide Battlesuit	1	245
XV25 Stealth Battlesuit	3-6	18

FAST ATTACK	MODELS/UNIT	POINTS/MODEL†
Kroot Hounds	4-12	6
Pathfinder Team	5-10	11
TX4 Piranhas	1-5	35
Tactical Drones	4-12	See Drones, opposite
Vespid Stingwings	4-12	14

DRONES	MODELS/UNIT	POINTS/MODEL**
MV62 Command-link Drone	N/A	10
MV33 Grav-inhibitor Drone	N/A	10
MV36 Guardian Drone	N/A	10
MV1 Gun Drone	N/A	10
MV17 Interceptor Drone	N/A	15
MV7 Marker Drone	N/A	10
MV8 Missile Drone	N/A	20
MV31 Pulse Accelerator Drone	N/A	10
MB3 Recon Drone	N/A	15
MV4 Shield Drone	N/A	15
MV52 Shield Drone	N/A	15
MV84 Shielded Missile Drone	N/A	30
MV71 Sniper Drone	N/A	20
MV5 Stealth Drones	N/A	10

HEAVY SUPPORT	MODELS/UNIT	POINTS/MODEL†
XV88 Broadside Battlesuit	1-3	45
TX7 Hammerhead Gunship	1	155
TX78 Sky Ray Gunship	1	100

DEDICATED TRANSPORTS	MODELS/UNIT	POINTS/MODEL†
TY7 Devilfish	1	75

FLYERS	MODELS/UNIT	POINTS/MODEL†
AX3 Razorshark Strike Fighter	1	100
AX39 Sun Shark Bomber	1	100

LORDS OF WAR	MODELS/UNIT	POINTS/MODEL*
KV128 Stormsurge	1	280

FORTIFICATIONS	MODELS/UNIT	POINTS/MODEL†
Tidewall Droneport	1	75
Tidewall Gunrig	1	125
Tidewall Shieldline	1	75
-Tidewall Defence Platform	0-1	75

Excluding wargear
**Including wargear*
† Excluding wargear and drones
†† Including wargear and drones
††† Including wargear but not drones

RANGED WEAPONS

	POINTS/WEAPON
Airbursting fragmentation projector	8
Burst cannon	8
Cluster rocket system	15
Cyclic ion blaster	18
Cyclic ion raker	0
Destroyer missile	0
Flamer	5
Fusion blaster	15
Fusion collider	5
Heavy burst cannon	0
Heavy rail rifle	25
High-output burst cannon	15
High-yield missile pod	25
Ion accelerator	15
Ion cannon	5
Ion rifle	5
Kroot gun	0
Kroot rifle	0
Longshot pulse rifle	0
Markerlight (Fire Warrior Shas'ui/other model)	5/0
Missile pod	15
Neutron blaster	0
Photon grenades	0
Plasma rifle	8
Pulse blastcannon	0
Pulse blaster	0
Pulse bomb	0
Pulse carbine	0
Pulse driver cannon	10
Pulse pistol	0
Pulse rifle	0
Quad ion turret	0
Rail rifle	10
Railgun	0
Seeker missile	5
Smart missile system	15
Supremacy railgun	0

MELEE WEAPONS

	POINTS/WEAPON
Equalizers	0
Honour blade	0
Kroot rifle	0
Krootox fists	0
Ripping fangs	0
Ritual blade	0

SUPPORT SYSTEMS

	POINTS/SYSTEM
Advanced targeting system (GHOSTKEEL, RIPTIDE and STORMSURGE)	20
Advanced targeting system (other model)	5
Counterfire defence system	10
XV8-02 Crisis Iridium battlesuit	10
Drone controller	5
Early warning override (GHOSTKEEL, RIPTIDE and STORMSURGE)	10
Early warning override (other model)	5
Homing beacon	20
Multi-tracker	5
Shield generator (STORMSURGE/other model)	30/10
Target lock (GHOSTKEEL, RIPTIDE and STORMSURGE)	10
Target lock (other model)	5
Velocity tracker (GHOSTKEEL, RIPTIDE and STORMSURGE)	10
Velocity tracker (other model)	5

TYRANIDS

HQ	MODELS/UNIT	POINTS/MODEL*
Broodlord	1	125
Hive Tyrant	1	155
Hive Tyrant with Wings	1	200
Neurothrope	1	95
Tervigon	1	200
Tyranid Prime	1	75

NAMED CHARACTERS	MODELS/UNIT	POINTS/MODEL**
Deathleaper	1	65
Old One Eye	1	220
The Red Terror	1	55
The Swarmlord	1	270

TROOPS	MODELS/UNIT	POINTS/MODEL*
Genestealers	5-20	15
Hormagaunts	10-30	6
Ripper Swarms	3-9	12
Termagants	10-30	5
Tyranid Warriors	3-9	21

ELITES	MODELS/UNIT	POINTS/MODEL*
Haruspex	1	170
Hive Guard	3-6	40
Lictor	1	32
Maleceptor	1	160
Pyrovores	1-3	28
Tyrant Guard	3-6	38
Venomthropes	3-6	33
Zoanthropes	3-6	45

FAST ATTACK	MODELS/UNIT	POINTS/MODEL*
Gargoyles	10-30	7
Mucolid Spores	1-3	22
Raveners	3-9	22
Spore Mines	3-9	10

HEAVY SUPPORT	MODELS/UNIT	POINTS/MODEL*
Biovores	1-3	50
Carnifexes	1-3	80
Exocrine	1	170
Mawloc	1	125
Screamer-Killers	1-3	105
Thornbacks	1-3	80
Toxicrene	1	150
Trygon	1	120
Trygon Prime	1	160
Tyrannofex	1	190

DEDICATED TRANSPORTS	MODELS/UNIT	POINTS/MODEL*
Tyrannocyte	1	65

FORTIFICATIONS	MODELS/UNIT	POINTS/MODEL*
Sporocyst	1	85

FLYERS	MODELS/UNIT	POINTS/MODEL*
Harpy	1	125
Hive Crone	1	155

RANGED WEAPONS	POINTS/WEAPON
Acid spray	5
Barbed strangler	10
Bio-electric pulse	0
Bio-electric pulse with containment spines	0
Bio-plasma	10
Bio-plasmic cannon	0
Bio-plasmic scream	0
Choking spores	0
Deathspitter	6
Deathspitter with slimer maggots	10
Devourer	4
Devourer with brainleech worms	10
Drool cannon	0
Flamespurt	0
Flesh hooks	3
Fleshborer	0
Fleshborer hive	0
Grasping tongue	0
Heavy venom cannon	20
Impaler cannon	10
Massive toxic lashes	0
Rupture cannon	20
Shockcannon	0
Spine banks	5
Spinefists (TERMAGANT/other model)	0/2
Spinemaws	3
Spore mine launcher	0
Spore node	0
Stinger salvo	0
Stranglethorn cannon	15
Tentaclids	0
Toxic lashes	0
Venom cannon	15

MELEE WEAPONS	POINTS/WEAPON
Acid maw	0
Biostatic rattle	0
Blinding venom	0
Bone mace	5
Boneswords	3
Claws and teeth	0
Crushing claws	10
Distensible jaws	0
Grasping talons	0
Lash whip and bonesword	3
Lash whip and monstrous bonesword	15
Massive crushing claws	20
Massive scything talons (TERVIGON and MALECEPTOR)	10
Massive scything talons (two or more pairs) (TRYGON and TRYGON PRIME)	30
Massive toxic lashes	0
Monstrous acid maw	10
Monstrous boneswords	20
Monstrous crushing claws	15

Excluding wargear
**Including wargear*
†† If models in this unit form a Brood Brother Weapons Team, there is no change
  in the unit's points cost.

MELEE WEAPONS	POINTS/WEAPON
Monstrous rending claws	0
Monstrous scything talons (CARNIFEX and HIVE TYRANT)	15
Monstrous scything talons (two pairs) (CARNIFEX)	15
Monstrous scything talons (two pairs) (HIVE TYRANT)	20
Powerful limbs	0
Prehensile pincer tail	0
Ravenous maw	0
Rending claws (GENESTEALER/other model)	0/2
Shovelling claws	0
Scything talons	0
Scything wings	0
Thresher scythe	5
Toxic lashes	0
Toxinspike	0
Wicked spur	0

BIOMORPHS	POINTS/BIOMORPH
Adrenal glands (MONSTER/other model)	5/1
Chitin thorns	5
Enhanced senses	10
Extended carapace	2
Spore cysts	10
Toxin sacs (TERMAGANT)	1
Toxin sacs (HORMAGAUNT)	2
Toxin sacs (TRYGON and TRYGON PRIME)	10
Toxin sacs (other models)	5
Tusks	10

GENESTEALER CULTS

HQ	MODELS/UNIT	POINTS/MODEL*
Abominant	1	110
Acolyte Iconward	1	60
Jackal Alphus	1	75
Magus	1	85
- Familiars	0-2	15
Patriarch	1	135
- Familiars	0-2	15
Primus	1	80

TROOPS	MODELS/UNIT	POINTS/MODEL*
Acolyte Hybrids	5-20	8
Brood Brothers Infantry Squad ††	10-20	5
Neophyte Hybrids	10-20	6

ELITES	MODELS/UNIT	POINTS/MODEL*
Aberrants	5-10	22
Biophagus	1	40
- Alchemicus Familiar	0-1	15
Clamavus	1	60
Hybrid Metamorphs	5-10	11
Kelermorph	1	80
Locus	1	45
Nexos	1	55
Purestrain Genestealers	5-20	17
Sanctus	1	60

FAST ATTACK	MODELS/UNIT	POINTS/MODEL*
Achilles Ridgerunner	1-3	40
Atalan Jackals	4-15	14 (Atalan Wolfquads are 20)
Cult Armoured Sentinels	1-3	30
Cult Scout Sentinels	1-3	30

HEAVY SUPPORT	MODELS/UNIT	POINTS/MODEL*
Brood Brothers Heavy Weapons Squad	3	6
Cult Leman Russ	1	130
Goliath Rockgrinder	1	90

DEDICATED TRANSPORTS	MODELS/UNIT	POINTS/MODEL*
Cult Chimera	1	65
Goliath Truck	1	50

FORTIFICATIONS	MODELS/UNIT	POINTS/MODEL**
Tectonic Fragdrill	1	80

RANGED WEAPONS	POINTS/WEAPON
Atalan incinerator	15
Autocannon (INFANTRY/other model)	10/15
Autogun	0
Autopistol	0
Battle cannon	20
Blasting charge	0
Bolt pistol	2
Cache of demolition charges	10
Clearance incinerator	30
Demolition charge	10
Eradicator nova cannon	15
Exterminator autocannon	30
Flamer	5
Frag grenades	0
Grenade launcher	5
Hand flamer	2
Heavy bolter (INFANTRY/other model)	10/15
Heavy flamer	15
Heavy mining laser	15
Heavy mortar	15
Heavy seismic cannon	15
Heavy stubber	5
Hunter-killer missile	5
Jackal sniper rifle	0
Lascannon (INFANTRY/other model)	15/20
Lasgun	0
Lasgun array	0
Laspistol	0
Liberator autostub	0
Mining laser	10
Missile launcher (INFANTRY/other model)	15/20
Mortar	10
Multi-laser	5

RANGED WEAPONS	POINTS/WEAPON
Multi-melta	25
Needle pistol	0
Plasma cannon	20
Seismic cannon	10
Shotgun	0
Silencer sniper rifle	5
Storm bolter	3
Twin autocannon	30
Vanquisher battle cannon	15
Web pistol	2
Webber	5

MELEE WEAPONS	POINTS/WEAPON
Bonesword	5
Chainsword	0
Cultist knife	0
Drilldozer blade	0
Familiar claws	0
Force stave	0
Heavy improvised weapon	30
Heavy power hammer	15
Heavy rock cutter	10
Heavy rock drill	15
Heavy rock saw	10
Hypermorph tail	0
Improvised weapon	0

MELEE WEAPONS	POINTS/WEAPON
Injector goad	0
Lash whip and bonesword	5
Locus blades	0
Metamorph claw	3
Metamorph talon	2
Metamorph whip	0
Monstrous rending claws	0
Power axe	5
Power hammer	5
Power maul	5
Power pick	10
Power sledgehammer	0
Purestrain talons	0
Rending claw(s)	0
Sanctus bio-dagger	0
Sentinel chainsaw	2
Toxin injector claw	0

OTHER WARGEAR	POINTS/WEAPON
Augur array	5
Cult icon	10
Cult vox caster	5
Dozer blade	5
Flare launcher	5
Spotter	5
Survey augur	5
Track guards	5

UNALIGNED FORTIFICATIONS

FORTIFICATIONS	MODELS/UNIT	POINTS/MODEL*
Aegis Defence Line	1	80
Chaos Bastion	1	170
Firestorm Redoubt	1	170
Fortress of Redemption	1	440
Imperial Bastion	1	150
Imperial Bunker	1	110
Imperial Defence Line	1	90
Macro-cannon Aquila Strongpoint	1	440
Plasma Obliterator	1	210
Skyshield Landing Pad	1	120
Vengeance Weapon Batteries	1-2	88
Void Shield Generator	1	200
Vortex Missile Aquila Strongpoint	1	470

RANGED WEAPONS	POINTS/WEAPON
Aquila macro-cannon	0
Battle cannon	20
Heavy bolter	15
Icarus lascannon	20
Plasma obliterator	0
Punisher gatling cannon	35
Redemption missile silo	0
Quad-gun	30
Quad Icarus lascannon	80
Twin Icarus lascannon	0
Vortex missile battery	0

* Excluding wargear
** Including wargear

FORGE WORLD POINTS VALUES

ADEPTUS ASTARTES

NAMED CHARACTERS	MODELS/UNIT	POINTS/MODEL**
Armenneus Valthex	1	90
Bray'arth Ashmantle	1	330
Carab Culln the Risen	1	400
Casan Sabius	1	185
Chaplain Ivanus Enkomi	1	100
Gabriel Angelos	1	195
Hecaton Aiakos	1	175
Lord Asterion Moloc	1	165
Lugft Huron	1	170
Magister Sevrin Loth	1	150
Tyberos the Red Wake	1	175

HQ	MODELS/UNIT	POINTS/MODEL*
Damocles Command Rhino	1	120

ELITES	MODELS/UNIT	POINTS/MODEL*
Relic Contemptor Dreadnought	1	105
Siege Dreadnought	1	80

FAST ATTACK	MODELS/UNIT	POINTS/MODEL*
Deathstorm Drop Pod	1	120
Land Speeder Tempest	1-3	60
Relic Javelin Attack Speeder	1	70

HEAVY SUPPORT	MODELS/UNIT	POINTS/MODEL*
Deimos Relic Predator	1	90
Deimos Vindicator Laser Destroyer	1	200
Land Raider Achilles	1	190
Land Raider Helios	1	205
Land Raider Prometheus	1	180
Relic Land Raider Proteus	1	210
Relic Sicaran	1	180
Relic Sicaran Arcus Strike Tank	1	175
Relic Sicaran Omega Tank Destroyer	1	200
Relic Sicaran Punisher	1	180
Relic Sicaran Venator	1	200
Rapier Weapons Battery Carrier	1	20
- Space Marine Gunners	2	15
Relic Whirlwind Scorpius	1	195
Tarantula Air Defence Battery	1-3	70
Tarantula Sentry Gun	1-3	20
Contemptor Mortis Dreadnought	1	105
Mortis Dreadnought	1	70
Relic Deredeo Dreadnought	1	150
Relic Leviathan Dreadnought	1	220

DESIGNATED TRANSPORT	MODELS/UNIT	POINTS/MODEL*
Infernum Pattern Razorback	1	80
Lucius Dreadnought Drop Pod	1	80
Terrax-pattern Termite	1	130

FLYER	MODELS/UNIT	POINTS/MODEL*
Fire Raptor Gunship	1	280
Storm Eagle Assault Gunship	1	230
Storm Eagle Assault Gunship – ROC Pattern	1	245
Xiphon Interceptor	1	110

LORDS OF WAR	MODELS/UNIT	POINTS/MODEL*
Astraeus Super-heavy Tank	1	500
Sokar Pattern Stormbird	1	2000
Thunderhawk Gunship	1	1350
Relic Cerberus Heavy Tank Destroyer	1	680
Relic Falchion Super-heavy Tank	1	790
Relic Fellblade Super-heavy Tank	1	690
Relic Mastodon Super-heavy Transport	1	915
Relic Spartan Assault Tank	1	320
Relic Typhon Heavy Siege Tank	1	720

RANGED WEAPONS	POINTS/WEAPON
Aiolos missile launcher	30
Air defence missiles	0
Anvillus autocannon battery	70
Arachnus heavy lascannon battery	75
Assault cannon	20
Bolt pistol	0
C-beam cannon	30
Castellum air defence missiles	20
Castellum battle cannon	55
Cyclone missile launcher	25
Cyclonic melta lance	60
Deathstorm cannon array	0
Deathstorm missile array	0
Demolisher cannon	0
Dreadhammer siege cannon	0
Dreadnought inferno cannon	25
Fellblade accelerator cannon	0
Frag grenade	0
Grav-flux bombard	65
Graviton blaster	15
Heavy bolter	15
Heavy flamer	15
Heavy neutron pulse array	0
Heavy plasma cannon	20
Helios launcher	0
Hellfire plasma carronade	50
Hellstrike battery	60
Hunter-killer missile	5
Infernus cannon	45

RANGED WEAPONS

RANGED WEAPONS	POINTS/WEAPON
Ironhail heavy stubber	5
Kheres assault cannon	25
Krak grenade	0
Lascannon	20
Las-ripper	30
Laser destroyer	60
Laser volley cannon	0
Magna-melta cannon	50
Meltagun	10
Missile launcher	20
Multi-melta	25
Neutron pulse cannon	0
Plasma blastgun	10
Plasma destroyer	40
Plasma eradicator	25
Predator autocannon	40
Punisher rotary cannon	0
Quad heavy bolter	60
Quad lascannon	80
Quad launcher	45
ROC missile launcher	0
Scorpius multi-launcher	40
Siege melta array	0
Skyreaper battery	45
Spectre pattern bolter	0
Storm bolter	3
Storm cannon array	50
Tempest salvo launcher	0
Thunderhawk heavy cannon	0
Turbo-laser destructor	0
Twin accelerator autocannon	0
Twin assault cannon	40
Twin autocannon	30
Twin avenger bolt cannon	0
Twin heavy bolter	30
Twin heavy flamer	30
Twin hellstrike launcher	50
Twin lascannon	40
Twin macro-accelerator cannon	120
Twin multi-melta	50
Twin volcano cannon	0
Twin volkite charger	10
Typhoon missile launcher	40
Vengeance launcher	20
Whirlwind castellan launcher	15
Xiphon missile battery	30

MELEE WEAPONS

MELEE WEAPONS	POINTS/WEAPON
Crushing tracks	0
Dreadnought chainfist (single/pair)	30/40
Dreadnought combat weapon (single/pair)	20/30
Leviathan siege claw (single/pair)	20/30
Leviathan siege drill (single/pair)	30/40
Seismic hammer	30
Termite drill	0

AUXILIARY EQUIPMENT

AUXILIARY EQUIPMENT	POINTS/WEAPON
Atomantic pavaise	40
Enhanced repulsor field	0

GREY KNIGHTS

LORDS OF WAR	MODELS/UNIT	POINTS/MODEL*
Thunderhawk Assault Gunship	1	1350

HEAVY SUPPORT	MODELS/UNIT	POINTS/MODEL*
Vortimer pattern Land Raider Redeemer	1	245

RANGED WEAPONS	POINTS/WEAPON
Flamestorm cannon	30
Hellstrike battery	60
Hunter-killer missile	6
Lascannon	25
Multi-melta	22
Storm bolter	3
Thunderhawk heavy cannon	0
Turbo-laser destructor	0
Twin heavy bolter	30
Twin psycannon	50

INQUISITION

NAMED CHARACTERS	MODELS/UNIT	POINTS/MODEL**
Inquisitor-Lord Hector Rex	1	110
Inquisitor-Lord Solomon Lok	1	75

HEAVY SUPPORT	MODELS/UNIT	POINTS/MODEL*
Inquisition Land Raider Prometheus	1	180

RANGED WEAPONS	POINTS/WEAPON
Flamestorm cannon	0
Hunter-killer missile	5
Multi-melta	22
Quad heavy bolter	60
Storm bolter	3

ADEPTUS CUSTODES

TROOPS

	MODELS/UNIT	POINTS/MODEL*
Custodian Guard with Adrasite and Pyrithite Spears	3-5	55
Sagittarum Custodians	3-5	50

ELITES

	MODELS/UNIT	POINTS/MODEL*
Aquilon Custodians	3-6	75
Contemptor-Achillus Dreadnought	1	160
Contemptor-Galatus Dreadnought	1	175

FAST ATTACK

	MODELS/UNIT	POINTS/MODEL*
Agamatus Custodians	3-6	100
Pallas Grav-attack	1	105
Venatari Custodians	3-6	55

HEAVY SUPPORT

	MODELS/UNIT	POINTS/MODEL*
Caladius Grav-tank	1	225
Telemon Heavy Dreadnought	1	200

DEDICATED TRANSPORT

	MODELS/UNIT	POINTS/MODEL*
Coronus Grav-carrier	1	265

FLYER

	MODELS/UNIT	POINTS/MODEL*
Ares Gunship	1	430
Orion Assault Dropship	1	500

RANGED WEAPONS

	POINTS/WEAPON
Achillus dreadspear	0
Adrasite spear	0
Adrastus bolt caliver	0
Adrathic devastator	5
Arachnus heavy blaze cannon	0
Arachnus magna-blaze cannon	0
Arachnus storm cannon	40
Galatus warblade	0
Iliastus accelerator culverin	25
Infernus firepike	10
Infernus incinerator	10
Kinetic destroyer	0
Lastrum bolt cannon	0
Lastrum storm bolter	0
Pyrithite spear	0
Spiculus bolt launcher	10
Spiculus heavy bolt launcher	0
Twin Adrathic destructor	15
Twin Arachnus blaze cannon	0
Twin Arachnus heavy blaze cannon	0
Twin Iliastus accelerator cannon	0
Twin las-pulser	30
Twin Lastrum bolt cannon	0
Twin plasma projector	15
Venatari lance	0

MELEE WEAPONS

	POINTS/WEAPON
Interceptor lance	0
Misericordia	3
Solerite power gauntlet	5
Solerite power talon	0
Tarsus buckler	5
Telemon caestus (single/pair)	30/40

OTHER WARGEAR

	POINTS/WEAPON
Galatus shield	0

ADEPTUS MECHANICUS

ELITES

	MODELS/UNIT	POINTS/MODEL*
Secutarii Hoplites	10-20	10
Secutarii Peltasts	10-20	9

DEDICATED TRANSPORT

	MODELS/UNIT	POINTS/MODEL*
Terrax-pattern Termite Assault Drill	1	130

RANGED WEAPONS

	POINTS/WEAPON
Arc lance	0
Arc pistol	5
Heavy flamer	0
Galvanic caster	0
Melta cutter	0
Phosphor blast pistol	3
Radium pistol	0
Storm bolter	3
Twin volkite charger	10

MELEE WEAPONS

	POINTS/WEAPON
Arc maul	5
Power sword	5
Taser goad	5

OTHER WARGEAR

	POINTS/WEAPON
Enhanced data-tether	5
Mag-inverter shield	0
Omnispex	5

* Excluding wargear
** Including wargear

ASTRA MILITARUM

ELITES	MODELS/UNIT	POINTS/MODEL*
Cyclops Demolition Vehicle	1-3	60
Hades Breaching Drill Squadron		
- Hades Breaching Drill	1	65
- Veterans	10	6

FAST ATTACK	MODELS/UNIT	POINTS/MODEL*
Artemia Pattern Hellhound	1-3	115

HEAVY SUPPORT	MODELS/UNIT	POINTS/MODEL*
Armageddon Pattern Basilisk	1-3	120
Armageddon Pattern Medusa	1-3	120
Carnodon	1	60
Colossus Bombard	1-3	155
Earthshaker Carriage Battery		
- Earthshaker Carriage	1-3	100
- Guardsman Crewman	4-12	5
Heavy Mortar Battery		
- Heavy Mortar	1-3	65
- Guardsman Crew	3-9	5
Heavy Quad Launcher Battery		
- Heavy Quad Launcher	1-3	95
- Guardsman Crew	3-9	5
Leman Russ Annihilator	1-3	130
Leman Russ Stygies Vanquisher	1-3	155
Malcador Annihilator	1	215
Malcador Defender	1	200
Malcador Heavy Tank	1	215
Malcador Infernus	1	315
Manticore Battery	1-3	135
Medusa Carriage Battery		
- Medusa Carriage	1-3	90
- Guardsman Crew	4-12	5
Rapier Laser Destroyer		
- Rapier Laser Destroyer	1	90
- Guardsmen Crew	2	5
Stygies Thunderer Siege Tank	1-3	135
Tarantula Battery	1-3	20

DEDICATED TRANSPORT	MODELS/UNIT	POINTS/MODEL*
Centaur Light Carrier	1	50
Gryphonne Pattern Chimera	1	65
Trojan Support Vehicle	1	105

FLYERS	MODELS/UNIT	POINTS/MODEL*
Arvus Lighter	1-3	115
Avenger Strike Fighter	1	165
Lightning Strike Fighter	1	135
Thunderbolt Heavy Fighter	1	125
Vendetta Gunship	1-3	95
Vulture Gunship	1-3	140

LORDS OF WAR	MODELS/UNIT	POINTS/MODEL*
Arkurian Pattern Stormblade	1	425
Crassus Armoured Assault Vehicle	1	200
Dominus Armoured Siege Bombard	1	590
Macharius Heavy Tank	1	400
Macharius Vanquisher	1	410
Macharius Vulcan	1	415
Marauder Bomber	1	260
Marauder Destroyer	1	180
Minotaur Artillery Tank	1	320
Praetor Armoured Assault Launcher	1	400
Valdor Tank Hunter	1	400

RANGED WEAPONS	POINTS/WEAPON
Artemia inferno cannon	0
Autocannon	15
Avenger bolt cannon	0
Battle cannon	20
Bolt pistol	2
Co-axial storm bolter	0
Colossus siege mortar	0
Cyclops demolition charge	0
Defensive heavy stubber	0
Demolisher cannon	20
Earthshaker cannon	0
Flamer	5
Frag grenade	0
Grenade launcher	5
Heavy bolter	15
Heavy flamer	15
Heavy mortar	0
Heavy quad launcher	0
Heavy stubber	5
Hellfury missile	15
Hellstrike missile	10
Hunter-killer missile	5
Inferno gun	0
Krak grenade	0
Lascannon	20
Laser destroyer	0
Lasgun	0
Lasgun array	0
Laspistol	0
Long-barrelled autocannon	15
Macharius battle cannon	0
Macharius vanquisher cannon	0
Macharius vulcan mega-bolter	0
Manticore missile	10
Medusa siege cannon	0
Medusa siege gun	0
Meltagun	10
Missile launcher	20
Multi-laser	5
Multi-melta	25
Multiple rocket pod	5
Neutron laser projector	0
Plasma blastgun	0
Plasma cannon	15
Plasma gun	10
Plasma pistol	5
Praetor launcher	0

* Excluding wargear
** Including wargear

RANGED WEAPONS	POINTS/WEAPON
Shotgun	0
Sky eagle rocket	10
Skystrike missile	15
Storm bolter	3
Stygies Vanquisher battle cannon	0
Twin assault cannon	40
Twin autocannon	30
Twin earthshaker cannon	0
Twin heavy bolter	30
Twin heavy flamer	30
Twin heavy stubber	10
Twin lascannon	40
Twin multi-laser	10
Twin punisher gatling cannon	70
Volkite caliver	15
Volkite culverin	30

MELEE WEAPONS	POINTS/WEAPON
Adamantium tracks	0
Chainsword	0
Melta-cutter drill	0
Power axe	5
Power fist	10
Power sword	5
Powerlifter	0

OTHER WARGEAR	POINTS/WEAPON
Cluster of heavy bombs	30
Cluster of hellstorm bombs	40
Cluster of tactical bombs	20

DEATH KORPS OF KRIEG

HQ	MODELS/UNIT	POINTS/MODEL*
Death Korps Death Rider Squadron Commander	1	45
Death Korps Field Officer	1	30
Death Korps Marshal	1	35

NAMED CHARACTERS	MODELS/UNIT	POINTS/MODEL**
Death Korps Marshal Karis Venner	1	65

TROOPS	MODELS/UNIT	POINTS/MODEL*
Death Korps Infantry Squad	10	6
Death Korps Grenadier Storm Squad*	5-10	7

ELITES	MODELS/UNIT	POINTS/MODEL*
Death Korps Commissar	1	20
Death Korps Death Rider Command Squadron	4	13
Death Korps Combat Engineer Squad*	5-10	7
Death Korps of Krieg Command Squad*	4	7
Death Korps Quartermaster Cadre		
- Quartermaster Revenant	1	50
- Medicae Servitor	2-4	5

FAST ATTACK	MODELS/UNIT	POINTS/MODEL*
Death Korps Death Rider Squadron	5-10	13

HEAVY SUPPORT	MODELS/UNIT	POINTS/MODEL*
Death Korps Heavy Weapons Squad	3	7
Death Korps Leman Russ Mars Alpha Battle Tanks	1-3	130

DEDICATED TRANSPORT	MODELS/UNIT	POINTS/MODEL*
Death Korps Centaur Light Assault Carrier	1	50
Death Korps of Krieg Storm Chimera	1	65

RANGED WEAPONS	POINTS/WEAPON
Acid gas bomb	0
Autocannon (INFANTRY/other model)	10/15
Battle cannon	20
Bolt pistol (COMMISSAR/other model)	0/2
Boltgun	2
Co-axial heavy stubber	0
Co-axial storm bolter	0
Conqueror battle cannon	25
Demolisher cannon	20
Demolition charge	5
Eradicator nova cannon	15
Executioner plasma cannon	15
Exterminator autocannon	30
Flamer	5
Frag grenade	0
Grenade launcher	5
Heavy bolter (INFANTRY/other model)	10/15
Heavy flamer (INFANTRY/other model)	10/15
Heavy stubber	5
Hot-shot lasgun	0
Hot-shot laspistol	0
Hunter-killer missile	5
Krak grenade	0
Krieg combat shotgun	1
Lascannon (INFANTRY/other model)	15/20
Lasgun	0
Lasgun array	0
Laspistol	0
Melta bomb	5
Meltagun (model with a Ballistic Skill of 4+/other model)	5/10
Missile launcher (INFANTRY/other model)	15/20
Mole launcher	20
Mortar	10
Multi-laser	5
Multi-melta	25

RANGED WEAPONS

	POINTS/WEAPON
Multiple rocket pod	5
Plasma cannon	20
Plasma gun (model with a Ballistic Skill of 4+/other model)	5/10
Plasma pistol	5
Punisher gatling cannon	35
Storm bolter	3
Twin heavy stubber	10
Twin lascannon	40
Vanquisher battle cannon	15

MELEE WEAPONS

	POINTS/WEAPON
Chainsword	0
Death Korps hunting lance	2
Medical scalpels	0
Power axe	5
Power fist	10
Power maul	5
Power sword	5
Savage claws	0

OTHER WARGEAR

	POINTS/WEAPON
Ablative storm armour and mine plough	10
Medi-pack	5
Memento mori	10
Platoon standard	5
Regimental standard	5
Storm armour and mine plough	10
Vox-caster	5

QUESTOR IMPERIALIS

LORDS OF WAR	MODELS/UNIT	POINTS/MODEL*
Acastus Knight Asterius	1	850
Acastus Knight Porphyrion	1	820
Armiger Moirax	1-3	155
Cerastus Knight-Acheron	1	520
Cerastus Knight-Atrapos	1	580
Cerastus Knight-Castigator	1	460
Cerastus Knight-Lancer	1	460
Questoris Knight Magaera	1	490
Questoris Knight Styrix	1	475

RANGED WEAPONS

	POINTS/WEAPON
Acheron flame cannon	0
Atropos lascutter	0
Autocannon	15
Castigator bolt cannon	0
Graviton crusher	0
Graviton singularity cannon	0
Helios defence missiles	45
Ironstorm missile pod	15
Karacnos mortar battery	0
Lascannon	20
Lightning cannon	0
Lightning lock	5
Moirax conversion beam cannon	15
Phased plasma-fusil	0
Rad cleanser	0
Twin conversion beam cannon	0
Twin heavy bolter	0
Twin magna lascannon	0
Twin rad-cleanser	0
Volkite chieorovile	0
Volkite culverin	0
Volkite veuglaire	5

MELEE WEAPONS

	POINTS/WEAPON
Cerastus shock lance	0
Hekaton siege claw	55
Moirax siege claw	0
Reaper chainfist	0
Reaper chainsword	30
Tempest warblade	0
Titanic feet	0

TITAN LEGIONS

LORDS OF WAR	MODELS/UNIT	POINTS/MODEL*
Reaver Battle Titan	1	4000
Warbringer Nemesis Titan	1	5000
Warhound Scout Titan	1	2000
Warlord Battle Titan	1	6000

DAEMON BOUND

ELITES	MODELS/UNIT	POINTS/MODEL*
Chaos Decimator	1	100

FAST ATTACK	MODELS/UNIT	POINTS/MODEL*
Greater Blight Drone	1	255
Blood Slaughterer of Khorne	1	180

LORDS OF WAR	MODELS/UNIT	POINTS/MODEL*
Greater Brass Scorpion of Khorne	1	600
Kytan Ravager	1	430

RANGED WEAPONS	POINTS/WEAPON
Bile maw	0
Blightreaper cannon	0
Butcher cannon	35

RANGED WEAPONS	POINTS/WEAPON
C-beam cannon	30
Decimator storm laser	25
Hellflamer	20
Impaler harpoon	0
Kytan gatling cannon	0
Scorpion cannon	0
Soulburner petard	60
Soulshatter bombard	0
Twin hellmaw blasters	0

MELEE WEAPONS	POINTS/WEAPON
Decimator siege claw (single/pair)	30/40
Great cleaver of Khorne	0
Hellcrusher claws	0
Plague probe	0
Slaughter blade	0

HELLFORGED

ELITES	MODELS/UNIT	POINTS/MODEL*
Hellforged Contemptor Dreadnought	1	105

HEAVY SUPPORT	MODELS/UNIT	POINTS/MODEL*
Hellforged Deredeo Dreadnought	1	150
Hellforged Land Raider Achilles	1	190
Hellforged Land Raider Proteus	1	210
Hellforged Leviathan Dreadnought	1	220
Hellforged Predator	1	90
Hellforged Rapier	1-3	20
- Chaos Space Marine Crew	N/A	10
Hellforged Scorpius	1	195
Hellforged Sicaran	1	180
Hellforged Sicaran Venator	1	200

DEDICATED TRANSPORT	MODELS/UNIT	POINTS/MODEL*
Terrax-pattern Termite Assault Drill	1	130
Hellforged Dreadclaw Drop Pod	1	130

LORDS OF WAR	MODELS/UNIT	POINTS/MODEL*
Hellforged Cerberus Heavy Destroyer	1	680
Hellforged Falchion	1	790
Hellforged Fellblade	1	690
Hellforged Mastodon	1	915
Hellforged Spartan Assault Tank	1	320
Hellforged Typhon Heavy Siege Tank	1	720

RANGED WEAPONS	POINTS/WEAPON
Bolt pistol	0
Boltgun	0
Butcher cannon	35
Butcher cannon array	75
C-beam cannon	30
Combi-bolter	3
Combi-flamer	10
Combi-melta	10
Combi-plasma	10
Demolisher cannon	0
Dreadhammer siege cannon	0
Dual malignatas saker	40
Ectoplasma battery	50
Ectoplasma blaster	10
Ectoplasma cannon	20
Fellblade accelerator cannon	0
Grav-flux bombard	65
Greater havoc launcher	20
Havoc launcher	5
Heavy bolter	15
Heavy flamer	15
Hellflamer	20
Infernal flamestorm cannon	30
Kharybdis storm launchers	0
Kheres assault cannon	25
Lascannon	25
Laser destroyer	60
Magna-melta cannon	40
Malignatas beam cannon	0
Malignatas beam laser	0
Melta cutter	0
Melta cutters	0
Meltagun	10
Multi-melta	25
Plasma destroyer	40
Predator autocannon	40

RANGED WEAPONS

RANGED WEAPONS	POINTS/WEAPON
Quad heavy bolter	60
Quad lascannon	80
Scorpius multi-launcher	40
Siege melta array	0
Skyreaper battery	45
Soulburner	30
Soulburner bombard	90
Soulburner ribaudkin	70
Storm bolter	3
Thermal jet array	0
Thermal jets	0
Twin accelerator autocannon	0
Twin autocannon	30
Twin heavy bolter	30
Twin heavy flamer	30
Twin lascannon	40
Twin multi-melta	50
Twin volcano cannon	0
Twin volkite charger	10

MELEE WEAPONS	POINTS/WEAPON
Blade struts	0
Eternal hunger	0
Hellforged chainclaw (single/pair)	30/40
Hellforged deathclaw (single/pair)	20/30
Hellforged siege claw (single/pair)	20/30
Hellforged siege drill (single/pair)	30/40
Infernal hunger	0
Termite drill	0

OTHER WARGEAR	POINTS/WEAPON
Hellfire veil	40

LORDS OF RUIN

NAMED CHARACTERS	MODELS/UNIT	POINTS/MODEL**
Zhufor the Impaler	1	120
Necrosius the Undying	1	135

HERETIC TITAN LEGIONS

LORDS OF WAR	MODELS/UNIT	POINTS/MODEL**
Chaos Reaver Battle Titan	1	4000
Chaos Warhound Scout Titan	1	2000
Chaos Warlord Battle Titan	1	6000

EYRINE CULTS

FLYERS	MODELS/UNIT	POINTS/MODEL*
Chaos Fire Raptor Assault Gunship	1	280
Chaos Hell Blade	1	100
Chaos Hell Talon	1	195
Chaos Storm Eagle Assault Gunship	1	230
Chaos Xiphon Interceptor	1	110

LORDS OF WAR	MODELS/UNIT	POINTS/MODEL*
Chaos Sokar Pattern Stormbird Gunship	1	2100
Chaos Thunderhawk Assault Gunship	1	1350

RANGED WEAPONS	POINTS/WEAPON
Balefire missiles	30
Baletalon shatter charges	0
Dreadstrike missiles	0
Havoc launcher	5
Hellstrike battery	60
Hellstrike missiles	50
Helstorm cannon	25
Lascannon	20
Pyrax incendiary bombs	0
Quad heavy bolter	60
Reaper battery	30
Soulstalker missile launcher	50
Thunderhawk cluster bombs	60
Thunderhawk heavy cannon	0
Turbo-laser destructor	0
Twin avenger bolt cannon	0
Twin heavy bolter	30
Twin lascannon	40
Twin multi-melta	50
Vengeance launcher	30
Warp-pulse bombs	0

CHILDREN OF THE WARP

NAMED CHARACTERS	MODELS/UNIT	POINTS/MODEL**
Cor'bax Utterblight	1*	230
Mamon Transfigured	1*	200
Uraka the Warfiend	1*	150

LORDS OF WAR	MODELS/UNIT	POINTS/MODEL**
Aetaos'rau'keres	1*	1500
An'ggrath the Unbound	1*	888
Scabeiathrax the Bloated	1*	777
Zarakynel	1*	666

* Excluding wargear
** Including wargear

QUESTOR TRAITORIS

LORDS OF WAR	MODELS/UNIT	POINTS/MODEL*
Acastus Knight Asterius	1	850
Acastus Knight Porphyrion	1	820
Cerastus Knight-Acheron	1	520
Cerastus Knight-Atrapos	1	580
Cerastus Knight-Castigator	1	460
Cerastus Knight-Lancer	1	460
Questoris Knight Magaera	1	490
Questoris Knight Styrix	1	475
War Dog Moirax	1-3	155

RANGED WEAPONS	POINTS/WEAPON
Acheron flame cannon	0
Atropos lascutter	0
Autocannon	15
Castigator bolt cannon	0
Graviton crusher	0
Graviton singularity cannon	0
Helios defence missiles	45
Ironstorm missile pod	15
Karacnos mortar battery	0
Lascannon	20
Lightning cannon	0
Lightning lock	5
Moirax conversion beam cannon	15
Phased plasma-fusil	0
Rad cleanser	0
Twin conversion beam cannon	0
Twin heavy bolter	0
Twin magna lascannon	0
Twin rad-cleanser	0
Volkite chieorovile	0
Volkite culverin	0
Volkite veuglaire	5

MELEE WEAPONS	POINTS/WEAPON
Cerastus shock lance	0
Hekaton siege claw	55
Moirax siege claw	0
Reaper chainfist	0
Reaper chainsword	30
Tempest warblade	0
Titanic feet	0

ASURYANI

NAMED CHARACTERS	MODELS/UNIT	POINTS/MODEL**
Irillyth	1*	150

HQ	MODELS/UNIT	POINTS/MODEL*
Wraithseer	1	115

TROOPS	MODELS/UNIT	POINTS/MODEL*
Corsair Reaver Band	5-15	10
Corsair Skyreaver Band	5-10	13

ELITES	MODELS/UNIT	POINTS/MODEL*
Shadow Spectres	3-10	27

FAST ATTACK	MODELS/UNIT	POINTS/MODEL*
Corsair Cloud Dancer Band	3-9	23
Hornet	1-3	65
Wasp Assault Walker	1-3	65

HEAVY SUPPORT	MODELS/UNIT	POINTS/MODEL*
Lynx	1	360
Warp Hunter	1	205

FLYERS	MODELS/UNIT	POINTS/MODEL*
Nightwing	1	95
Phoenix	1	210

LORDS OF WAR	MODELS/UNIT	POINTS/MODEL*
Cobra	1	600
Phantom Titan	1	2400
Revenant Titan	1	2000
Scorpion	1	700
Skathach Wraithknight	1	470

RANGED WEAPONS	POINTS/WEAPON
Aeldari missile launcher	20
Blaster	15
Brace of pistols	5
Bright lance	20
Cloudburst missile launcher	0
D-bombard	0
D-cannon	40
D-flail	0
D-impaler	0
Dark lance (INFANTRY/other model)	15/20
Deathshroud cannon	45
Dire pulsar	0
Dissonance cannon	20
Dissonance pistol	5
Flamer	5
Fusion gun	10
Haywire launcher	0
Hornet pulse laser	25
Inferno lance	60

RANGED WEAPONS

RANGED WEAPONS	POINTS/WEAPON
Lasblaster (ANRATHE)	7
Lynx pulsar	0
Nightfire missile array	0
Phoenix missile array	0
Phoenix pulse laser	0
Prism blaster	5
Prism rifle	15
Pulsar	0
Scatter laser	10
Shardcarbine	0
Shredder	10
Shuriken cannon	10
Shuriken catapult	0
Sonic lance	60
Splinter cannon (INFANTRY/other model)	10/15
Starcannon	15
Sunburst grenades	0
Twin bright lance	40
Twin Scorpion pulsar	0
Twin shuriken cannon	20
Twin shuriken catapult	0
Twin starcannon	30
Voidstorm missile launcher	0
Wraithcannon	0

MELEE WEAPONS	POINTS/WEAPON
Ghostspear	0
Spar-glaive	0
Titanic feet	0
Titanic stride	0
Titanic wraithbone fists	0
Void sabre	10
Wraith glaive	0

DRUKHARI

HEAVY SUPPORT	MODELS/UNIT	POINTS/MODEL**
Reaper	1	150
Tantalus	1	400

NECRONS

FAST ATTACK	MODELS/UNIT	POINTS/MODEL*
Canoptek Acanthrites	3-9	55
Canoptek Tomb Sentinel	1	150
Canoptek Tomb Stalker	1	130

HEAVY SUPPORT	MODELS/UNIT	POINTS/MODEL*
Sentry Pylon	1-3	80
Tesseract Ark	1	210

FLYER	MODELS/UNIT	POINTS/MODEL*
Night Shroud	1	210

LORDS OF WAR	MODELS/UNIT	POINTS/MODEL*
Gauss Pylon	1	500
Seraptek Heavy Construct	1	660

FORTIFICATIONS	MODELS/UNIT	POINTS/MODEL*
Tomb Citadel	1	730

RANGED WEAPONS	POINTS/WEAPON
Cutting beam	0
Exile cannon	0
Focussed death ray	35
Gauss annihilator	0
Gauss cannon (VEHICLE)	5
Gauss exterminator	50
Heat cannon	75
Particle beamer (TESSERACT ARK)	0
Tesla arc	0
Tesla cannon	13
Tesla destructor	0
Tesseract singularity chamber	0
Twin gauss slicers	0
Twin tesla destructor	0

MELEE WEAPONS	POINTS/WEAPON
Automaton claws	0
Voidblade	0

OTHER WARGEAR	POINTS/WEAPON
Gloom prism	5
Teleportation matrix	10

ORKS

HQ	MODELS/UNIT	POINTS/MODEL**
Warboss on Warbike	1	100

HEAVY SUPPORT	MODELS/UNIT	POINTS/MODEL*
Battle Wagon with Supa-kannon	1	210
Big Trakk	1	150
Grot Mega-tank	1	95
Grot Tanks	4-8	35
Meka-Dread	1	250

DEDICATED TRANSPORTS	MODELS/UNIT	POINTS/MODEL*
'Chinork' Warkopta	1	85

LORDS OF WAR	MODELS/UNIT	POINTS/MODEL*
Gargantuan Squiggoth	1	360
Kill Tank	1	420
Kustom Stompa	1	960

RANGED WEAPONS	POINTS/WEAPON
Belly gun	50
Bigbomm	0
Big lobba	30
Big shoota	5
Big zzappa	5
Boom kanister	5
Bursta kannon	0
Dakkagun	0
Deffgun	0
Deffkannon	0
Flakka gunz	15
Gaze of Mork	50
Giga shoota	5
Grot sponson	10
Grotzooka	10

RANGED WEAPONS	POINTS/WEAPON
Kannon	15
Killkannon	15
Kustom mega-blasta	10
Lifta-droppa	0
Lobba	20
Rack of rokkits	25
Rattler kannon	0
Rokkit launcha	10
Shoota	0
Shunta	5
Skorcha	15
Slugga	0
Stikkbomm	0
Supa-gatler	0
Supa-kannon	0
Supa-lobba	50
Supa-rokkit	5
Supa-skorcha	30
Twin big shoota	10
Zzap gun	15

MELEE WEAPONS	POINTS/WEAPON
Attack squig	0
Big choppa	5
Deff rolla	20
Grabbin' klaw	5
Huge tusks	0
Mega klaw (one/each subsequent mega klaw)	50/30
Rippa klaw (one/each subsequent rippa klaw)	20/5
Wreckin' ball	5

OTHER WARGEAR	POINTS/WEAPON
'Ard case	0
Grot riggers	5
Reinforced ram	5
Rokkit bomm racks	15

T'AU EMPIRE

NAMED CHARACTERS	MODELS/UNIT	POINTS/MODEL**
Shas'o R'alai	1	115
Shas'o R'myr	1	130

ELITES	MODELS/UNIT	POINTS/MODEL*
XV107 R'varna Battlesuit	1	430
XV109 Y'vahra Battlesuit	1	395
XV9 Hazard Support Team	1-3	70

FAST ATTACK	MODELS/UNIT	POINTS/MODEL*
Tetra Scout Speeder	2-4	45

FLYERS	MODELS/UNIT	POINTS/MODEL*
Barracuda AX-5-2	1	200
Tiger Shark AX-1-0	1	530
Tiger Shark Fighter-bomber	1	340

LORDS OF WAR	MODELS/UNIT	POINTS/MODEL*
KX139 Ta'unar Supremacy Armour	1	750
Manta Super-heavy Dropship	1	2000

DRONES		POINTS/WEAPON
Blacklight Marker Drones	n/a	10
DX4 Technical Drones	2-10	20
DX-6 Remora Stealth Drone	1-6	60

* Excluding wargear
** Including wargear

RANGED WEAPONS	POINTS/WEAPON
Burst cannon	8
Cyclic ion blaster	18
Double-barrelled burst cannon	4
Defensive charge	0
Fletchette pod	0
Fusion blaster	15
Fusion cascade	20
Fusion eradicator	0
Heavy rail cannon	0
High intensity markerlight	0
High yield missile pod	25
Ion cannon	0
Ionic discharge cannon	0
Long-barrelled burst cannon (BARRACUDA/other model)	10/0
Long-barrelled ion cannon	0
Markerlight	0
Missile pod	15
Nexus meteor missile system	30
Phased ion gun	0
Phased plasma-flamer	0
Plasma rifle	8
Pulse carbine	0
Pulse rifle	0
Pulse submunitions cannon	0
Pulse submunitions rifle	0
Pulse ordnance multi-driver	0
Rail rifle	10

RANGED WEAPONS	POINTS/WEAPON
Seeker missile	5
Skyspear missile rack	0
Smart missile system	15
Swiftstrike burst cannon	25
Swiftstrike railgun	5
Tri-axis ion cannon	25
Twin swiftstrike burst cannon	40

MELEE WEAPONS	POINTS/WEAPON
Crushing feet	0

SUPPORT SYSTEMS	POINTS/SYSTEM
Advanced targeting system (Y'vahra and R'varna)	20
Advanced targeting system (other model)	5
Counterfire defence system	10
Drone controller	5
Early warning override (Y'vahra and R'varna)	10
Early warning override (other model)	5
Multi-tracker	5
Shield generator (Y'vahra and R'varna)	40
Shield generator (other model)	10
Target lock (Y'vahra and R'varna)	10
Target lock (other model)	5
Velocity tracker (Y'vahra and R'varna)	10
Velocity tracker (other model)	5

TYRANIDS

HQ	MODELS/UNIT	POINTS/MODEL*
Malanthrope	1-3	135

FAST ATTACK	MODELS/UNIT	POINTS/MODEL*
Dimachaeron	1	210
Meiotic Spores	3-9	20
Sky-slasher Swarms	3-9	15
Tyranid Shrikes	3-9	24

HEAVY SUPPORT	MODELS/UNIT	POINTS/MODEL*
Stone Crusher Carnifex Brood	1-3	90

LORDS OF WAR	MODELS/UNIT	POINTS/MODEL*
Barbed Hierodule	1	460
Harridan	1	760
Hierophant Bio-titan	1	2000
Scythed Hierodule	1	410

RANGED WEAPONS	POINTS/WEAPON
Barbed strangler	10
Bio-acid spray	0
Bio-cannon	0
Bio-plasma	10
Bio-plasma torrent	0
Boneswords	3
Deathspitter	6

RANGED WEAPONS	POINTS/WEAPON
Devourer	4
Dire bio-cannon	0
Flesh hooks	3
Spinefists	2
Spinemaws	3
Venom cannon	15

MELEE WEAPONS	POINTS/WEAPON
Bio-flail	0
Bone mace	5
Claws and teeth	0
Grasping tail	0
Grasping talons and thorax spine maw	0
Lash whip pods	0
Lash whip and bonesword	3
Massive scything talons	0
Monstrous scything talons	0
Rending claws	2
Scything talons	0
Sickle claws	0
Thresher scythe	5
Wrecker claws (single/pair)	10/15

BIOMORPHS	POINTS/BIOMORPH
Adrenal glands	1
Toxin sacs	5

MISCELLANEOUS POINTS VALUES

GELLERPOX INFECTED

UNIT	MODELS/UNIT	POINTS/MODEL**
Vulgrar Thrice-Cursed	1	70
The Vox-Shamblers	3	9
Glitchlings	4	5
The Hullbreakers	3	35
Cursemites	4	5
Eyestinger Swarms	4	5
Sludge-Grubs	4	5

ELUCIDIAN STARSTRIDERS

UNIT	MODELS/UNIT	POINTS/MODEL**
Elucia Vhane	1	50
Nitsch's Squad	6	7
Knosso Prond	1	28
Larsen van der Grauss	1	25
Sanistasia Minst	1	20

IMPERIUM

NAMED CHARACTERS	MODELS/UNIT	POINTS/UNIT**
Ephrael Stern and Kyganil of the Bloody Tears	2	125
Valerian and Aleya	2	200

BLACKSTONE FORTRESS

UNIT	MODELS/UNIT	POINTS/UNIT**
Amallyn Shadowguide	1	55
Ambull	1	75
Aradia Madellan	1	45
The Archivist	1	90
Black Legionnaires	2	28
Borewyrm Infestation	1-2	15
Chaos Beastmen	4	26
Chaos Ogryn	1	70
Cultist Firebrand	1	35
Cultists of the Abyss	7	40
Daedalosus	1	55
Dahyak Grekh	1	40
Espern Locarno	1	35
Gotfret de Montbard	1	40
Guardian Drone	1	90
Janus Draik	1	45
Negavolt Cultists	4	50
Neyam Shai Murad	1	55
Obsidius Mallex	1	130
Pious Vorne	1	30
Rein and Raus	2	40
Rogue Psyker	1	35
Spindle Drones	4	65
Taddeus the Purifier	1	55
Traitor Guardsmen	7	40
Traitor Commissar	1	55
UR-025	1	45
Ur-Ghul	1	15
X-101	1	25

INDOMITUS SET

SPACE MARINES	MODELS/UNIT	POINTS/MODEL**
Assault Intercessor Squad	5-10	19 (Sergeant with plasma pistol is 24)
Bladeguard Ancient	1	85
Bladeguard Veteran Squad	3	35
Eradicator Squad	3	40
Firestrike Servo-turret	1-3	90 (Firestrike Servo-turret with twin las-talon is 130)
Invader ATV	1-3	80 (Invader ATV with multi-melta is 85)
Judiciar	1	85
Outrider Squad	3	45
Primaris Captain	1	105
Primaris Chaplain	1	85
Primaris Chaplain on Bike	1	130
Primaris Lieutenant	1	90

NECRONS	MODELS/UNIT	POINTS/MODEL**
Canoptek Doomstalker	1	130
Canoptek Reanimator	1	110
Canoptek Scarab Swarms	3	15
Cryptothralls	2	20
Lokhust Heavy Destroyers	1-3	70
Necron Warriors	10-20	12
Overlord	1	90
Plasmancer	1	80
Royal Warden	1	80
Skorpekh Destroyers	3	40
- Plasmacyte	0-1	15
Skorpekh Lord	1	130